+ADVANCED PRAISE +

"If you are seeking vivid examples, proven strategies and practical advice on the toughest challenge organizations confront – namely, how to find new ideas, implement them successfully and effectively sustain them – +Change is an essential read! Whether you're an entrepreneur who wants to get big, a CEO who wants to avoid stagnation or a non-profit executive who seeks to make a deeper difference, +Change belongs in your leadership library – that is, after you read it!"

Mark C. Crowley, Author "Lead From The Heart
21st Century Leadership for the 21st Century"

" +Change is a game changer to improve personal and organizational effectiveness. Moe tackles the challenges as it relates to communications, innovation and leadership. Rather than the fluff of other best selling "thought leaders", Moe brings valuable and thought provoking ideas to the table. This book should be read and reread to firmly grasp the essential concepts."

Lavie Margolin, Career Coach, Author "Lion Cub Job Search – Practical
Job Search Assistance for Practical Job Seekers"

"Change in organizations is inevitable and it's also one of the most difficult things to do. We talk about it a lot, but the implementation of any change effort often doesn't achieve what we envisioned. Moe Glenner has the answer: +Change: Genesis of Innovation. By using the proven formulas and techniques in this book, you can embrace the changes to help your organization move forward with more confidence and less fear. A must read."

Susan C. Foster, Executive Coach and author of the best seller
"It's Not Rocket Science: Leading, Inspiring and
Motivating Your Team To Be Their Best"

"A great read that provides real, practical advice whether you're a team of 5 or 50,000. *+Change* delivers just the right strategies to show how almost any team can find new ideas, implement them and then sustain them."

Michael A. Bonventre, *Operations Manager, Rapid Drug Test Systems*

"I gained much from Moe Glenner's insights and wisdom. Two important lessons that I applied are to make sure that communications follows the CHART formula: clear, honest, appreciative, relevant and timely, and how to harness my innate creativity"

Colonel (Ret.) Jill Morgenthaler,
Author, Leadership Expert, International Speaker

"Everyone in business today desires innovation, but very few ever achieve it. Moe Glenner gives us everything we need – including strategies, tactics and real-world tips – to master change, ideate and drive innovation in our organizations."

Kevin Kruse, *New York Times Bestselling Author*
"Employee Engagement 2.0"

"Moe's new book, *+Change: Genesis of Innovation* takes a bold step beyond Selfish Altruism: Managing & Executing Successful Change Initiatives. Moe's new book delves into how to use change + ideas to accelerate innovation. Focusing on the keystones of Creativity, Communication and Innovation, this book will help guide you to release preconceived expectations and unlock true potential, success and profits. Create a ROI that is both personal and powerful. Invest your time with *+Change*. You will not be disappointed."

John Chappelear, *Founder & President of Changing the Focus*

"A great book by Moe with his unique perspective on leadership in change. It has simple yet powerful ideas you can use as a business consultant or as a leader for innovative problem solving. It shows how ideation can be a good tool to build a progressive organization and helps you to understand the real innovation for business."

Vivek Naik, *Coach and Trainer to business owners*

"When Moe speaks, we should listen. Why? Because his track record on leading innovation, creativity and meaningful change for business organizations speaks for itself. Moe's latest work gives us insights into how change works best.

I have never been a fan of the statement that "change is the only constant". This is tantamount to saying that change is the only thing that matters. Change only matters if it produces outcomes that are valued by organizations and their stakeholders. Everything else is noise. Moe gives us a roadmap to understand how we can harness the power of creativity and innovation to make changes that create real business value. His approach is practical and insightful.

Any pilot will tell you that if you take off without a clear destination, you might run out of fuel before you land. The map matters. As a professional pilot himself, Moe knows that if "something goes contrary to plan, I can't just pull over to the nearest cloud".

Change for change-sake is disruptive to business operations. Change for the sake of creative advancement and the ideation of great new strategies – well that's a powerful way to take flight. As he has so eloquently stated, "By unlocking the creativity and the previously unrealized and non-communicated ideas, we unlock the growth potential and profits."

Randy Shattuck, *Chief Thinker & Strategist – The Shattuck Group*

"To be successful in the future, organizations cannot just embrace change, they need to drive change and this book clearly identifies the core elements for creating sustainable positive change. Moe Glenner has developed several new groundbreaking ideas in the areas of creativity, ideation, change management and innovation that can help any organization successfully implement proactive change as a strategic advantage."

John Spence
– one of the top 100 business thought leaders in America

"Change is a popular 'buzz-word' in business today. But managing and even leading organizational change are not natural-born skill sets. It requires a different mindset and a tangible, innovative process to bring it to life. In his groundbreaking new book +Change, Moe Glenner transcends the 'change-trend' and digs deep into why it's needed, how to creatively craft it, and most importantly, how change drives innovation to benefit your organization and your people. Buy this book, highlight it, write all over it and dog-ear the pages!"

David Arvin CSP, The Visibility Coach, Top-Selling Author, "It's Not Who You Know, It's Who Knows YOU! (Classified Press)

"Moe Glenner provides the world a fresh, insightful and often humorous view of the inevitable events and changes in our world that affect us all. From change to creativity to innovation, +Change: Genesis of Innovation provides us a new pattern of thought that can help everyone – from the office to the home. His use of aviation as an analogy is a great way of applying the theories. This book will stand the test of time!"

Erika Armstrong, Author of A Chick in the Cockpit, business owner, professional pilot columnist for Disciples of Flight and NYC Aviation.

"A nifty, no-nonsense dive into the dynamics of idea generation. Any Leadership Team that is serious about sustainable change will be instantly inspired by this book!"

Achim Nowak, Author of The Moment and Infectious: How to Connect Deeply And Unleash the Energetic Leader Within

"Moe Glenner's book provides insights on the key principles of change and innovation. For entrepreneurs or business leaders at the forefront of organizational growth, +Change is a treasure trove of case studies and industry showcases."

Kevin Knebl, CMEC Social Selling & Relationship Marketing Specialist Int'l Speaker/Author/Trainer and Executive Coach

PLUS

CHANGE

GENESIS OF **INNOVATION**

Published by
LID Publishing Inc.
31 West 34th Street, Suite 7004,
New York, NY 10001, US

One Adam Street, London
WC2N 6LE

info@lidpublishing.com
www.lidpublishing.com

A member of:

www.businesspublishersroundtable.com

Printed in the United States
ISBN: 978-0-9860793-4-4

Cover and page design: Caroline Li

PLUS CHANGE

GENESIS OF **INNOVATION**

Moe Glenner

LONDON   MONTERREY
MADRID   SHANGHAI
MEXICO CITY   BOGOTA
NEW YORK   BUENOS AIRES
BARCELONA   SAN FRANCISCO

CONTENTS

ACKNOWLEDGMENTS

Just as no man is an island, this work was assisted by a cast of many. And while simply mentioning them here is not nearly sufficient, I would like to start by showing my appreciation and recognizing their contributions.

A big thank you, for agreeing to be interviewed and their comments included, to (in no particular order): John Surma, Jim Vrtis, David Nihill, Yuri Cataldo, Jim Schrager, John Correnti, Lance Fleming, Garen Smith, Eric Summa, Wally Pasko, Mark Keller and Murray Crane. As senior executives and advisors, I am especially appreciative of the time they generously gave to help influence this book.

My appreciation also to the following people I've spoken with and interviewed on my past Leadership Takeoff talk show: Jared Korpal, Wes Kautzmann, Chaim Shapiro, Andrew Tarvin, Bruce Day, Alice Lerman and Yuri Cataldo (again). Their leadership insights as well as feedback have provided additional color and flavor to this work as well. Thank you.

I would also like to thank Dave Lerman for his continuing support and encouragement. And while he would demur from such public praise, I cannot think of a finer example of class and leadership, as well as acute business acumen. Thank you.

More thanks to all those who graciously gave of their time to review, comment and critique throughout the process of writing and editing. And also thank you to a cast of many others (including those whom I have inadvertently not mentioned), who continue to inspire, motivate and educate. Your contributions are most valuable and appreciated.

I would also like to thank (if this were the Academy Awards, my microphone would be cutting out about now. . . . (silence). . . . .) the fantastic team at LID Publishers: Sara, Andy, Elisa, Amrita, Martin and the rest of the team. You guys are simply the best. Huge thank you!

Finally, I owe an incredible debt of gratitude to Sheila and the kids (Daniel, Kaila, Eliana and Akiva). While they say behind every great man (a bit hesitant to refer to myself as such), there is an even greater woman, I don't feel that even remotely captures Sheila's contributions. I don't do and can't do what I do without your continuing love, patience and support. And especially to Eliana (my now 3-year-old) who has been especially inspirational (through her boundless creative energy (aka trouble).) The Biggest Thank You! (and xoxoxoxo forever!)

✝ FOREWORD ✚

By Jane Sunley, CEO of Purple Cubed; UK best-selling author of Purple Your People and It's Never OK to Kiss the Interviewer; co-author of 20/20: 20 Great Lists by 20 Outstanding Business Thinkers

When Moe Glenner asked me to write this forward, I didn't have to think twice before I agreed to do it. Moe is a man with something important to say. And his timing is so right.

The fashionable executive acronym of the moment is VUCA, shorthand for volatility, uncertainty, complexity, and ambiguity; in other words 'the world is pretty nuts right now'.

VUCA rolls four distinct types of challenges into one, it asks myriad questions, requiring a variety of responses. By the time you've worked out what's happening and what to do about it, your strategy is shot, you're onto another set of challenges and VUCA is hailed as root cause for lack of growth, profitability, innovation, return on investment, service...

Well, the world is nuts, it has been for quite some time and that's not going to change any day soon. So what we really need, in a sea of 'books about change', is someone who's going to simplify and demystify this nuts old world of business.

In his last book *(Selfish Altruism Booklocker, 2012)*, Moe kick started the important discussion around the components of both successful and unsuccessful change initiatives. He has now expanded on this by demonstrating that there's far more to change than most people think. People need to know this stuff.

In said VUCA environments, everyone wants to 'innovate' and fast, but so many actually divert their time and effort into being creative; coming up with the ideas. Because it's enjoyable, fun, engaging and gets everyone excited. This means not enough effort goes into the actual innovation (delivering on those ideas). That's because this part is much harder to do, it's sometimes tedious, detail-focused, expensive, open to failure and not without its risks. Sometimes it takes too long.

Far too many of the brilliant creative ideas people have had tragically never made it to fruition.

By exploring the dynamic between change, creativity and innovation, Moe helps the reader to navigate their intersection and the interrelationships between them. This is essential reading for anyone challenged by creating sustainable and evolving business change as well as demonstrating tangible return on investment from the creative process.

Jane Sunley, August 2015

✝INTRODUCTION✝

My previous book, *Selfish Altruism: Managing & Executing Successful Change Initiatives* (Booklocker, 2012), started the important discussion regarding the components of both unsuccessful and successful change initiatives. It also introduced two critical components of any change initiative: Communication and personal return on investment (PROI). Essentially, one could be self-serving and still benefit the greater good (in our case, benefitting the organization counts as such).

After all the media attention had subsided, I realized there was certainly a great deal more to change than simply the components and the motivators. If we stop and think about any initiative, personal and/or professional, something – and frequently, many things – need to change for it to be sustainably successful.

But what is the genesis of this change and how do we even know that things should change? How does change permeate our desire to discover and capitalize on our innate creativity? How does change ultimately affect whether or not we can sustainably innovative? Since life will frequently take us to the intersection of creativity, change and innovation, how do we successfully navigate this junction?

None of these important questions were directly answered in *Selfish Altruism* (if at all) but they certainly need to be addressed if we are to de-isolate change; and de-isolate, we must. In my (not so) humble opinion, change cannot only be that thing to which we refer when the going gets tough. After all, how we look at change through the prism of creativity and innovation, ultimately affects our ability to embrace and welcome it as well. And while there are many fine works on change management, creativity and/or innovation, there are precious few (if any) that discuss the interrelationships between all of them.

This book will address and attend to all of these critical questions as well as focus significant attention on creativity and how we can be more creative; finding new ways of establishing and internalizing practical processes for change; and finally broadening our horizons toward sustainable innovation. Note: I use sustainable in its literal definition: 'standing the test of time' rather than the more recent definition of 'environmentally friendly' (not that there's anything wrong with the latter).

While change is a key component, it isn't, nor should it be, the only component. When I first started writing this sequel to *Selfish Altruism*, I was merely looking to fill in remaining gaps and perhaps add more color and analogies. Thus, my original working title was *Changistics – Innovative Change Leadership for the Bold Pursuers*. As my research/discovery and writing progressed, I realized that change by itself was too small a vessel to capture leadership and/or innovation appropriately. In other words, my own working title forced my direction to shift beyond simply another exploration of change.

At about the same time, we started a limited run of public workshops titled Creativity for Profitability. The purpose was to show individuals and organizations that fostering an environment of creativity had a tangible ROI, as well as how to foster and accelerate enhanced creativity. While we only held a few of these workshops, the response was fantastic and some of the exercises used found their way into this book. From the feedback and further exploration, a creativity roadmap emerged. And like all maps, there are multiple roads leading in multiple directions ending at multiple destinations.

This forced a much closer look at what actually comprised sustainable innovation. After all, if life is one of constant motion, then we must always be moving forward to succeed. Standing still is, by definition, moving backwards. Thus, my 'aha!' moment emerged and I developed the ICI Formula for Sustainable Innovation: Ideation + Change = Innovation. This became the basis and guide for the entire work. I was also fortunate enough to interview many senior leaders and former senior leaders of both large and small organizations to gain their insights of these principles in action. Their insights are mentioned throughout the book and I am thankful for their contributions (see acknowledgments, page 10).

Of course, one needs to explore how we think of ideas, the environments most conducive to coming up with them, the creativity necessary to inspire them and, finally, how best to select from them. In the book, I refer to this map as the 'Nifty-Nine Creative Principles'. The destination reached will depend on the principles used and their order (purely subjective). Regardless, the vehicle for travelling to this destination will be our heightened sense of creativity.

Moving on to change, the concept of Changistics and its components make a grand entrance. We explore the takeaways from Changistics through the prism of general aviation, expanded learnings of *Selfish Altruism* and through real-life examples. Also, communication is given outsized importance in this section. Certainly, communication is important in ideation and innovation too and I don't intend to downplay its importance there. However, without excellent communication (CHART – clear, honest, appreciative, relevant, timely), all change initiatives are doomed to fail, sometimes spectacularly. While this book is not just focused on change, we cannot and should not ignore its importance. And we won't.

Finally, we talk about innovation, our desired end result. How do we create and maintain a culture of innovation? Through what models can an organization strive to create an innovative environment? Can we use tools not specifically designed for innovation (5M+1: Man, material, machine, measurement, method and environment, and so on) to help inspire and propel forward our innovative selves? These and other questions are directly confronted and addressed in the innovation section (page 207).

Essentially, this book speaks about leadership. I rely heavily on my knowledge and experience as a professional general aviation (GA) pilot and use many analogies and mnemonics to drive home specific points. As a pilot, the overriding goal is to land the plane safely; if it happens to be at its intended destination, it's a bonus. As a pilot, despite meticulous and comprehensive planning, I fly in the weather I find, not the weather for which I planned. Every flight is an exercise in change leadership. After all, if something goes contrary to plan, I can't just pull over to the nearest cloud.

For personal and professional success, better leadership needs to be exhibited. I would like to believe that this book will help initiate the conversation about, and help develop and sustain, creative leadership, change leadership, communications leadership and innovation leadership. There should be no limits to what you can achieve. Always remember: The sky is not the limit – it's just the beginning.

To you and your success,

Moe

THE ONLY CONSTANT

IN LIFE IS CHANGE

We've all heard this story before: Something is wrong, brainstorming sessions are called for and survived, politicking and raw power prevails. Change is then instituted, often without input or feedback from those affected. Resistance mounts until finally the change dies a sudden death or lingers awkwardly and painfully until put out of its misery at a later date. Our brutal takeaway: Change stinks!

Almost always, the fact that something or someone has to change is indicative of problems and/or issues. We almost never hear of implemented change when things are going well, do we? But was it the change itself that caused a lasting impression or could it also have been flawed processes starting with perception of the problem and including how the problem was dealt with?

Yet, the only thing we can count on is that things will change and that we will likely change. If we consider this to be true, might it not make sense to learn to embrace change? And if we embrace change, perhaps it won't be quite so painful, detested or feared. Perhaps then, change won't be relegated to times when something has gone wrong, but strategically employed as a means to drive sustainable innovation.

However, before we can embrace change, we need to understand better not only the change process but also everything necessary to ideate and communicate why we might need to, or desire to, change. This is the heart of +Change.

For any change, understanding how and why we got to this point is critical to ideating, planning and executing an effective and sustainable change. And sustainable change is something for which we should all be striving. After all, if the enacted change is only temporarily successful and/or effective, was it really worthy of the considerable time, effort and resources expended to enact it?

If we can assume that we have identified the actual problem (more on this later), then we now need to devise a solution. While it might be easy to think of solutions instantly, inevitably the best solutions will arise out of individual and/or collective creative efforts. Unfortunately, this is easier said than done.

We are truly our own worst enemies when it comes to creative thought, especially in the corporate arena. When we typically think of creativity, do we hark back to our school days with its requisite arts and crafts? Or do we leave the creativity to our mental perceptions of stereotypical 'creative-types', whose job it is to be creative? Actually, we are all quite creative and creativity will, at

By unlocking the creativity and the previously unrealized and non-communicated ideas, we unlock growth potential and profits.

times, manifest itself by playing a metaphorical game of 'peek-a-boo' within our routine stream of consciousness. There is truly an endless reservoir of creative thought just waiting to be tapped into, harnessed, utilized and maximized. If this doesn't seem likely, or if the skeptic in you is waiting to jump in, I can provide some initial muscle for your inner creativity that is waiting patiently for its reintroduction.

I design, and frequently lead, private on-site workshops with the express purpose of accelerating organizational innovative and creative potential leading to infinite growth potential. While this may sound like a mouthful, the concept is surprisingly simple: by unlocking the creativity and the previously unrealized and non-communicated ideas, we unlock growth potential and profits. These workshops are highly interactive and involve a series of exercises, which illustrate what people, and organizations, do wrong, along with error-reversing, cost-saving and profit-generating creativity concepts.

How is this done and why is it critically important?

Many corporations, ranging from the multinational companies GE, HP and 3M to many mid-size organizations, have invested in creativity training. The reported ROI has been quite good (Sylvania reported an ROI of 2,000% from one creativity course provided to several thousand of its employees - $20 for each $1 spent). Others reported 60% increases in patentable concepts (GE); savings of more than $5 million (DuPont); and 300% increase in viable ideas (PPG) (Wall

Street Journal, HP 2000 *Annual Report, Igniting Innovation Through the Power of Creative Thinking – David Tanner.)*

Creativity training can indeed be quite profitable, so why doesn't every organization make the investment? Many companies that bill themselves as progressive do indeed make an investment not only with creativity training but other soft skills training as well. Perhaps the question should really be phrased in terms of progression: Why aren't more companies willing to be progressive?

Among my clients, I have two organizations that are large, privately owned, multinational players in the plastics industry. Each of these organizations has annual revenues exceeding $2 billion. Both organizations are similar in many aspects of their operations and in their private ownership. Both organizations have also developed a fanatical loyalty to their employees, that is reciprocated by extremely low staff turnover rates coupled with strong employee loyalty to the organization.

Yet, these organizations are vastly different regarding progression.

One company's senior leadership is stuck in its ways and can, at times, be quite resistant to change. Certainly, the organization's continued viability relies on its fantastic customer service and other factors, but certain critical changes remain taboo. These changes range from the continued use of a very outdated legacy computer system to senior leadership's resistance to new soft skills engagement programs and ongoing communication breakdowns within, and between, departments. Having attended several executive meetings, I can personally attest to the common concern of almost everyone regarding addressing these issues and, ultimately, future viability.

The irony is that senior leadership acknowledges that changes must be made but struggles with moving forward and executing them. Much of this struggle is attributed to the sometimes painful nature of change and natural resistance to possible pain and/or the pain itself. These leaders' frequent mantra echoes the refrain "now is not the right time for these initiatives".

The other company is much more willing to make changes, even radical changes, within the organization. New initiatives are researched, decided on and executed without undue resistance. While its customer service is also renowned, its soft skills investments and communication throughout the organization are also enviable.

The difference between these companies is also what separates the corporations moving forward from those that are moving backwards. It might not be readily apparent, but unless the change-resistant company becomes more willing not only to adapt but to allow for significant change, its long-term viability is in question. To this company's credit, a few executives have started to pay more attention to change management and related initiatives. However, even these initiatives are given relatively low priority and are sacrificed on the altar of 'timing'. It remains to be seen if these initiatives will ever be successfully implemented and carried over to the entire organization.

What this company and others sometimes fail to realize is that ideas are the real corporate currency with dollars, pounds or euros being the net result. I would adamantly argue, based on everything we know about companies and what makes them succeed or fail (Jim Collins' publications *Good to Great and Built to Last* are phenomenal supporting resources), that the levels of ideation and change tolerance are directly reflected on the bottom line.

Looked at in another light, we can express these concepts formulaically:

SYSTEMATED IDEAS = INCREASED PROFITABILITY

Corporation Life = Constant Motion = Ideas + Change = Innovation
= Moving Forward
= Reduced Costs
= Increased Efficiencies
= Infinite Growth
= Increased Profitability
ICI = Ideas + Change = Innovation

This formulaic expression of corporate life and success will serve as the organizational basis for the remainder of this work. It is also the sequential order for continued viability and profitability within any corporate initiative. And while the focus is organizationally directed, the takeaways also apply to personal change.

We start with 'Idea', from which everything originates. Every business initiative, beginning with the founding of the organization itself, starts with an idea. Someone thinks of a way to support themselves, to sell something, market something, provide a needed service, provide a better service, design a product, and so on. Without a continuous supply of ideas, organizations stagnate, and a stagnant

organization's long-term viability is very much in question. We must systematically create ideas and an idea pipeline, aggregate and select from them (without bias)
and then successfully implement them. When we're done we must have a process
for continuously replenishing and refreshing the idea pipeline and its flow.

This is not an easy task, especially with companies that have been successfully
utilizing their existing systems. After all, they made it this far without systemized ideation, why implement it now? Furthermore, many of these companies
have formal and informal employee suggestion mechanisms to access ideas; isn't
that enough? I'll answer that question with another question: Are you able to
utter the words "suggestion box/email" without rolling your eyes in skepticism
and cynicism?

To put this in even clearer perspective, consider the following scenario: Bill, a
mid-level manager, suggests a fantastic idea. This game-changing idea will require
relatively little capital outlay and can be implemented fairly easily. Essentially, it
is the closest thing to a 'no-brainer'. At the same time, Jack, the company's vice
president, suggests an idea that, while good, doesn't have the same potential as
Bill's. If only one idea can be chosen, whose idea is likely to prevail?

Without systemized ideation, good and great ideas are not communicated, much
less realized. Without this system, idea bias is part of the selection process leaving
the best ideas not implemented. Can you, or your organization, sustain growth
within this status quo?

We will then continue to 'Change'. Any implemented idea will require some type
of change. Regardless if this is a change in thought, process, service, product or
personnel, our ability to plan, communicate and execute this change is critical
to continued creative and innovative success. If we fail in the change portion of
this initiative, continued idea inspiration will be significantly more difficult. We
need to understand the dynamics of change better ('Plan', 'Communicate' and
'Execute') and then harness these dynamics to achieve our desired result.

There is a misconception regarding change and, more specifically, our supposed
fear of it. We repeatedly hear it, "People are afraid of change"; "He's/she's afraid
to change"; "They just don't want to change", and so on. If we consider change
more closely, it isn't the change itself that generates the fear and impedes our
progress. It is the fear of the unknown that scares most of us.

Consider this scenario: You are holding the winning $400 million lottery ticket in this week's drawing. Your life is about to change and perhaps quite significantly. Are you afraid of this change? Most likely, you're not even thinking about the change and you most certainly are not going to be impeded in claiming your winnings even if there are some unknown or unspecified fears. Essentially, in all the excitement, we don't perceive any misgivings as actual fear.

So it is fair to say that if we can eliminate, mitigate and/or alleviate our fear of the unknown by making it less unknown, then we will certainly be less hesitant and might even embrace change. Of course, how we actually get there will be the subject of later discussion.

Our desired result from any change is 'Innovation'. While there are many different and diverse definitions, I prefer to define it simply as the successful execution of something new. It could be new to us, new to our team or new to our organization. It could be a completely novel thing or something that is radical; a true game-changer. It doesn't matter if it's a tweak or a radically different approach; if it is successfully executed, it is still an innovation.

Innovation relies first on 'Idea' and then on 'Change' to reach fruition. History is littered with examples of great ideas that failed the change portion (plan, communicate, execute), only to be resurrected later by others who were able to navigate the change process successfully. Were the originators innovators? While, in a technical sense, they were innovators, they were not able to profit from their own innovations. It is not enough to ideate; we must also be able to master change if we are to profit from our creativity.

So let's take a closer look at the components of systemized ideation, beginning with 'Idea'.

IDEA

IDEA GENERATION

We'll begin with a simple exercise using nothing but a brick and five minutes of your time. When the countdown timer begins, the task is to list all the ways in which the brick could be used. The first few answers should be relatively easy; it could be used to build a building, a wall, a deck, perhaps as a paper-weight. But can you think of any other uses? At this point we will put on our thinking caps and struggle to find other uses and perhaps think of one or two more. When the five minutes are up, we will congratulate ourselves on a job well done and look with pride at our lists.

But we're really nowhere close to completion. Let's set the stopwatch for a further five minutes, but this time, the challenge is that you must think of at least 50 ways to use this brick. There is no time to consider protesting or even judging; it's 'just the ideas ma'am' – apologies to Joe Friday (*Dragnet*, Warner Brothers, 1954). It doesn't matter if the uses are practical or not, whatever idea pops up, write it down. Unlike the initial five minutes, where the time elapsed long after you finished thinking of uses, you are likely to be feverishly writing down ideas when the proverbial buzzer sounds. You look down at your list and think of even more ideas. Among these ideas are all sorts of uses, including those that you previously judged impossible, impractical, unethical or perhaps even illegal. Some of these ideas necessitated changing the form of the brick (for example, grinding it up, fusing it together with other bricks, crushing it), others constituted weaponry (using it as a projectile, as a club, something to be dropped on someone).

Other ideas are likely to have pushed the 'boundaries' further still (spaceship, space module, medicinal uses, and so on).

Let's now think beyond the brick in its obvious form. Did we ever consider a brick of chocolate or cheese? What thoughts or ideas are inspired by thinking about food? What memories are suddenly brought to the forefront? Are there any ideas hiding in them?

So what just happened here? How did we go from six or seven ideas to well over 50 ideas? When there was no time limit, we thought of all the same things, but before they could be formed into an active conscious idea, our subconscious minds judged them and eliminated them from consideration, leaving only those conventional 'tried-and-tested' ideas. But when we forced the issue, by making it a requirement that 50 ideas were generated, our brains interpreted the command, as a "why the hell not?" command. Suddenly, the subconscious barrier was removed and every thought became a good idea. There was no issue with an idea being a stupid one or even appearing stupid. All we needed was 50 ideas, regardless of any other criteria. And with those 50 ideas, we are now able to address what needs to be changed in ways other than the usual 'tried-and-tested' methods. We can even perhaps realize a new method or procedure that will help propel us (and our organization) forward. Our result can be truly innovative if only we allow ourselves to bring our ideas forward.

Of course, it doesn't have to be a brick that can inspire. In the crowded bottled water marketplace, where is the real differentiation? What could be more mundane than water? Yuri Cataldo, founder and CEO of IndigoH2O and a theatre professor at the University of Indiana, begs to differ. His distinctive blue glass bottles of water have been featured at the Oscars, Emmys and MTV Music Awards as part of the exclusive gift baskets given to the presenters and special guests. They can also be found at selected Whole Foods stores.

While working to identify some personal health issues, he discovered the benefits of natural alkaline water. After testing and research, including the use of glass (instead of the prevalent plastic) and adopting the aesthetically pleasing blue color, he was ready to launch. He was able to look at water and see something others couldn't see which, in turn, allowed him to fill a gap in the market. During my conversation with Yuri, he offered this advice to would-be innovators: "After you have a product, test the hell out of it, including determining who the realistic customers would be. In other words, take action – stop thinking about it, just get it down. After determining the practicalities of cost and pricing, a quality product will sell itself through word of mouth (and helped with directed marketing). Also, keep experimenting."

As an example of unrealized innovation, Yuri mentioned the friend who had had an innovative fruit soda idea, but chose to not act on it, despite spending two years talking about it. Ultimately, success is about taking action. Thus, the lesson to anyone contemplating change or embarking on an innovative path is that it's great to think and plan, but without tangible action, nothing happens.

This is a classic example of divergent thinking. When we employ our conscious to divert from the normal operating modes, whether through suspension of the 'stupid-barrier' or other methods, we unlock much more of our brain's potential. The difficult part is training our brains and subconscious to divert from the norm and to allow these previously repressed ideas and notions to move forward.

Ideas are very much like a tree with multiple large branches leading to a higher number of smaller branches which lead to an almost infinite number of twigs and leaves. Our starter problem, necessitating the idea generation, is the trunk and each category of idea or thought becomes another large branch from

When we employ our conscious to divert from the normal operating modes, whether through suspension of the 'stupid-barrier' or other methods, we unlock much more of our brain's potential.

which the other thoughts, memories and inspirations expand outward. A tree is the ideal metaphor for another important reason: growth. Just as a tree never stops growing, our inspired ideas never stop growing. The only things standing in the way of growth are artificial barriers, the most prevalent one being the 'stupid barrier'.

I have seen the 'stupid' barrier appear over and over again, whether it is in the boardroom, the meeting room or even the informal brainstorming sessions that are so ubiquitous throughout the corporate world. Nobody wants to look stupid, especially in the eyes of their subordinates, colleagues and superiors. When someone offers an 'unconventional idea', the judging begins immediately. "That will never work"; "We can't afford that"; "That's not practical"; "They'll never go for that"; "What were you thinking!?"

In essence, this is the litmus test of good leadership. Good leadership allows for a diverse and disparate flow of ideas without prejudging. Good leadership doesn't immediately disparage or attack non-conforming ideas simply for the sake of ego or conformity. Good leadership actively encourages all ideas (and thus actively works to neutralize the team's individual 'stupid barriers' to allow for all and any ideas to see the light of day and be considered appropriately).

Eric Summa is CEO of Repellex and several other growing, innovative companies. Repellex is at the forefront of animal repellent technologies. His company, which specializes in infusion of hot peppers into plants prone to being consumed by animals, is expecting growth of more than 50% this year. In our conversation, Eric expressed amazement about the ongoing tolerance of mediocrity and negativity within organizations today.

His priority is finding the right people. "These are people with a desire to learn and adapt, regardless of background; people who are curious and love to discover. When there is a whiff of negativity or a feeling of 'can't-do', my job as a leader is to recognize the cycle of negativity and step in to break it." He stressed that while he seeks to continue inspiring a positive atmosphere, it's not at the expense of honest communication. 'Pie in the sky' communication only works if that is reality. Otherwise, all it accomplishes is a rapid diminishment of trust.

Through his commitment to staying positive and fostering open communication of business strategy and its goals, Eric's companies are, unsurprisingly, realizing and exceeding their growth trajectories.

But what happens where negative cycles are not broken and this leadership litmus test fails? Imagine being the person that just proposed what you considered to be a groundbreaking idea. But as soon as you proffered this game-changing suggestion, it was shot down in flames. How are you feeling right now? How likely are you to offer up another idea? How likely are you even to speak up again in this meeting? Now let's say that there are a few others that just observed your 'Sopwith Camel' of an idea being shot down by the 'Red Barons' in the room (apologies to Peanuts® and Snoopy; *The World War I Flying Ace*). How likely is it that these observers will offer any idea that isn't already conforming to the conventional norms? Will they risk being shot down as well? Will they fear looking stupid for even offering an idea that is outside the expected thought processes?

I recall my initial Six Sigma training, which comprised an in-house group of various managers and executives striving to earn a Six-Sigma Green Belt. This group of 16 was divided into two groups of eight and led by a moderator. The moderator was tasked with ensuring that the proper processes were being followed, not only in the Six Sigma processes, but even in the idea generation processes.

One of the initial challenges given to the teams was to list all the areas in which the company excelled and those in which improvement was needed. The moderator did state that there should be no judging of the ideas at this stage but, as you recall, there were a few executives sprinkled within these groups. While executives are not the only ones prone to quick judgment, their time is self-perceived to be at a premium, creating the artificial necessity to judge ideas as they're presented and perceived. Unfortunately, the ensuing exercise was quite predictable.

Someone commented that the company was risk-adverse, a statement immediately challenged by one of the executives. The moderator didn't intervene and correct the executive regarding not judging any ideas at this stage. The result: all remaining ideas were now only put forward by the other executives. If we set aside the moderator's failure to intervene, this exercise can be seen as a replica of virtually every brainstorming session in the corporate world today. It has become an exercise for the dominant and/or popular voices with all other voices muted for fear of looking stupid and/or being shot down publicly.

There is a school of thought, that argues being immediately critical of ideas helps refine the discussion and leads to better ideas and the most viable solution. I don't argue with this notion in itself, rather its timing. I agree that all suggested ideas should be assessed critically in the quest for the most viable, pursuable

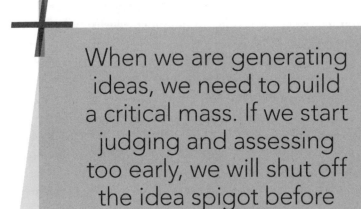

> When we are generating ideas, we need to build a critical mass. If we start judging and assessing too early, we will shut off the idea spigot before reaching this mass.

ideas; just not at this early stage. When we are generating ideas, we need to build a critical mass. If we start judging and assessing too early, we will shut off the idea spigot before reaching this mass. We might never know what ideas are now not being put forward (for fear of being shot down) or subsequently realized. By not judging, assessing or offering constructive criticism during the 'idea-generation phase', we allow for the building of a critical mass of ideas and achieve the maximum engagement and number of idea-offerings from those involved.

Fear is perhaps one of the most powerful and debilitating emotions in business as in life. We fear for our jobs, prestige and any requisite authority contained within. We fear looking stupid, saying anything stupid, taking risks or even communicating an idea that hasn't been officially sanctioned and approved by those higher up the ladder, and/or by the legal department. Above all, we fear failure and its potential consequences. Therefore, we need to do everything possible to mitigate fear during the idea generation phase.

Many companies suffer a self-inflicted dearth of generated ideas and innovations in processes and/or products. These same companies pay lip-service to the notion of thinking differently and rewarding risk takers, but when someone actually takes them up on the offer, the reaction is swift and adverse. Is it any surprise, then, that these companies have an almost empty ideas pipeline? And with an empty ideas pipeline, there can be only be accidental innovation, not a culture of innovation.

I recall an internal consulting position I took in the early 2000s with an established third-party logistics company (name withheld to protect the guilty). At my orientation, I was handed a copy of Gary Hamel's outstanding book, *Leading the Revolution* (Harvard Business School Press, 2000) and was informed that I would be responsible (with others) for innovating business processes. I celebrated the notion of experimenting with different ideas and methods in the normally staid logistics arena.

It wasn't long before I had an opportunity to test that notion. We were asked by a large international company to analyze and suggest ways to improve their supply chain. When the analysis was complete, I was asked to give a client presentation with the findings and suggestions. The struggle began the minute I started putting together the PowerPoint slides for the presentation, setting out the suggested course of action. I was informed that the slides had to be in a certain format, with no omissions, and that the suggested course of action had to be what the senior management (of the logistics company) had pre-ordained (namely, taking advantage of empty space in their existing warehouse locations); analysis and client needs be damned.

At first, I attempted to persuade and convince my superiors that we didn't need 15 slides on the history of our company and all the services we offered. I further attempted to use the 'innovation card' to explain my slide format, which differed from the established slide deck. All this was unsuccessful. Finally, I stated that, since I was the lead on the project, I would present the analysis and suggestions in a format of my choosing. If they didn't like it, they could remove me from the project and then present whatever they wanted. While this bordered on insubordination, I felt my mission was to lead innovation and that I needed to pressure resisters to go along with it.

At the client presentation, the client executives were impressed with not only the bold, clean format of the slides but with the suggested actions as well. The proposed suggestions were the best for the client company, even if it meant they wouldn't be using our pre-packaged solutions. The suggestions offered annual savings in excess of $10 million and the opportunity for us to be the lead consultants in their implementation. At the presentation's conclusion, I was asked to return to give a more detailed implementation presentation.

Sadly, I was never given the chance. Upon my return to the office, I was reprimanded for not using the official company slide deck and for not suggesting the pre-ordained ('in the box') solution. It made no difference that the presentation was enthusiastically received and that we had a real opportunity for significant consulting revenue. I had strayed from the 'box', and for that I needed to be flogged. After exhausting my efforts to persuade anyone in senior management, we agreed to part ways. I was particularly perturbed about being misled regarding 'leading the revolution' and/or innovation initiatives.

This logistics company struggled and stagnated for nearly ten years after this before eventually becoming better proponents of change, primarily due to competitive forces. In the interim, few people in this logistics company were willing to offer up new ideas. They had seen what had happened to me (and to others who dared to think differently) and were afraid of the consequences of repeating my 'audacious' attempt to innovate. How many great and forward-thinking initiatives were never realized because of this silence? How would they ever even know?

The lesson: If you intend to be innovative and creative don't just say that's what you want. You must be willing to accept that the innovation and creativeness will change established processes and that the ultimate result will be rewarding. You must be willing to encourage and listen for these ideas without adverse reaction and/or consequence. You must be willing to accept limited initiative failures as learning opportunities and continue to encourage experimentation. In other words, don't talk the talk if you're not going to walk the walk.

There can be no doubt that harnessing our innate creativity is critical to ensuring future corporate viability, organizational growth and profitability. But how do we get there, aside from parroting that almost meaningless phrase, "we have to think outside the box"? And how do we integrate creativity, which is highly subjective into our standard business operating processes, which are highly objective entities?

When faced with a challenge, either personally or professionally, the first step is recognizing that the challenge requires action. This recognition (or detection) is not so easily accomplished. We are creatures of comfort who crave stability. As such, even if the status quo isn't optimal, we at least understand its parameters and learn to cope. It truly is 'the devil we know', and somehow, even if we subconsciously recognize that things are not right, we'll allow ourselves to think that it's at least ok for now.

When faced with a challenge, either personally or professionally, the first step is recognizing that the challenge requires action.

For all of us, at least some of the time, denial is a primary self-defense mechanism. If we can just close our eyes and click our red-ruby shoes together three times, we'll be home and safe in no time. If we can just pretend and/or fool ourselves into thinking that our problems are not really problems or that they're not so bad, then our problems disappear and we will be able to carry on.

Except that the problem doesn't really go away. Despite our best efforts to deny that there is a problem and/or that the problem requires action, it remains as a present and viability-threatening danger. Thus, the first step in creativity integration is acceptance of a problem or issue that would necessitate a creative solution. For some organizations, the problem might be simply staying relevant in a world in which rapid innovation and change is the everyday *modus operandus*. For others the problem might be something more insidious such as process breakdowns, runaway costs or shrinking margins and/or markets.

This acceptance must be more than an acknowledgement of the problem; it must be accompanied by a realization that the problem is a clear and present threat to the viability of the enterprise. It must also be recognized that the problem will not go away by itself without the persistent and deliberative efforts of the team. And it must be affirmed that the mentality of "that's the way we did it before, the way we're doing it now and the way we'll continue to do it" will be discarded at the door. In other words, to remain healthy and viable, the enterprise must undertake successful and enduring change. And like any process, this change will require prudent and skillful management if it stands a fighting chance of eliminating or mitigating the problem at hand.

We will be revisiting change management, its key components and how creativity is integral to the process later in the book, so simply acknowledging and paying proper attention to the concept of change management is sufficient for now. At this point, we need to understand better the creative process and the specific barriers that prevent us from fully harnessing its corporate rehabilitative powers.

While there are almost endless components to the creative process, I strongly believe that there are nine primary principles and that everything else falls into one of these.

> In other words, to remain healthy and viable, the enterprise must undertake successful and enduring change. And like any process, this change will require prudent and skillful management if it stands a fighting chance of eliminating or mitigating the problem at hand.

These Nifty-Nine principles to the creative process are (in no particular order):

1. Release the endorphins
2. Separate idea generation from idea evaluation
3. Always test assumptions
4. Avoid patterned thinking
5. Create new perspectives
6. Minimize negative thinking
7. Take (prudent) risks
8. Get lost!
9. Turn out the lights

These principles are not mutually exclusive. Often, there are other principles influencing a primary principle. In many ways, our earlier experiment with the brick exemplifies many of these principles. Let's take a closer and more detailed look.

PRINCIPLE 1
RELEASE
THE ENDORPHINS

Organizations struggle with finding the right team-building and team-maintaining formulas. Many companies believe that, by emphasizing the team and teamwork through repetition of overused mantras (for example, "there is no I in team"), and the strategic posting of team-orientated inspirational posters, that a culture of teamwork will somehow evolve and be maintained.

While most people in an organization strive to be contributing members of the successful team, without true engagement and addressing of personal goals/motivators, the true benefits of teamwork will remain elusive. There are many diverse methods for building lasting engagement and the resulting culture of teamwork, but encouraging a culture of creativity and innovation should rightfully be a priority.

But while we will later work through many important principles of creativity to help our team be more creative and innovative, there is another important piece to this puzzle and that is taking ourselves so darn seriously.

I've been fortunate enough to have the opportunity to be part of, and observe, many different teams at many different levels. Some of these teams were sports-orientated; others were at a project team level, while others still were at senior management and executive levels. At times, many of these teams exhibited virtually every form of dysfunction known to man. One time, I even witnessed a physical fight between team members, requiring the immediate summoning of security. Certainly, these teams were teams in name only and definitely didn't foster a culture of engagement, creativity or innovation. We could spend a significant amount of time dissecting these dysfunctional teams and harping on about what went wrong. But we won't, because, after all, negativity breeds negativity.

I would rather focus on those teams that fostered a genuine spirit and culture of teamwork and engagement. Since these teams varied greatly in their make up and express purpose of being, it's necessary to identify and focus on a primary shared attribute: the ability of members not to take themselves too seriously.

This ability is not to be confused with an overall lack of seriousness. The people in these teams took their responsibilities very seriously and were determined to have a successful outcome. What they didn't do was take themselves too seriously. In other words, they were able to laugh at themselves and laugh together as a team.

In a conversation with David Nihill, founder of FunnyBizz (where business meets humor) and bestselling author of *Do you Talk Funny?* (2015), David affirmed the tangible positive impact that humor has on creativity. Organizations that embrace creativity and allow people to be themselves, by not forcing them to adopt

> While most people in an organization strive to be contributing members of the successful team, without true engagement and addressing of personal goals/motivators, the true benefits of teamwork will remain elusive.

different personas at work, create an environment of openness and accelerated creativity. He explained: "We should no longer have to separate our Facebook selves from our LinkedIn selves. Organizations that don't foster this environment lose out on the innate creativity that people exhibit away from work."

Ultimately, all business relies on the human element of forging and maintaining relationships and almost all of us love to be entertained. If we can create an environment in which people can be themselves and not feel they have to 'walk on eggshells', creativity and innovation will be unleashed.

David talked further about the role that leadership plays in the formation and continuation of the creative environment. Through leadership by design, wherein senior leadership communicates and acts in a less formal fashion, the example is set for the rest of the organization. As an example, David mentioned Dick Costolo, former CEO of Twitter and former stand-up comedian. In a recent interview entitled *"Twitter's CEO used to be a professional comedian – here's how improv comedy helped him be a better leader"* (Smith, David, *BusinessInsider*, 25 February, 2015), Dick talked about being "in the moment" and listening. Via the power of always answering with "yes, and . ..", senses and thus ideas, are more ably propelled forward. After all, every idea needs to be nurtured, even if the initial reaction is that the idea will not or cannot possibly work.

> If we can create an environment in which people can be themselves and not feel they have to 'walk on eggshells', creativity and innovation will be unleashed.

There is even a role for humor in change initiatives, David posits, provided that the humor is focused on the process of change, rather than the specific pain points or reasons for resisting the change. While we'll talk about change later, it is important to realize just how versatile humor can be, from organizational, leadership, change and innovation perspectives.

As children, our laughter was free-flowing. Most of us had very few worries, few responsibilities and there was no risk to laughing out loud. Then we grew up and took on all our increased responsibilities and the ensuing quest for the corner office. Our professional titles grew to outsized importance. We segregated personal fun from professional activities. Laughter was relegated to social events and banished from the conference rooms. We strived to become industrial and corporate legends with all of the implied and requisite seriousness. But with all that seriousness, we forgot that being good teammates and team leaders requires more than just professional competence; it requires us to be personable and relatable.

There is something to a relaxed, contagious social laughter that has a unique bonding effect. "Laugh and the world laughs with you" is more than just cliché; it is also a basis for team engagement. This doesn't require us to become stand-up comedians or even necessarily the life of the party; however, it does require us to let down our personal guards, and to refrain from being so caught up in job titles and ambitions. If we can take ourselves a bit less seriously, we will be able to laugh at ourselves, and more importantly, laugh with our team.

But how does laughter, even team laughter, relate to creativity and to building a culture of creativity and innovation?

When we laugh, the physical muscular exertions involved set in motion the sudden release of endorphins. Endorphins are the brain chemical that is directly related to feeling good. When we feel good, we usually find ourselves in a more relaxed state than previously.

We'll discuss later the creativity-inducing benefits of being in a relaxed state when we turn out the lights. Anything that puts us in a more relaxed and more content state serves the purpose of lulling our subconscious minds and bypassing the 'stupid' filter (our internal barrier to ideas and thoughts that we otherwise might consider stupid). When we take ourselves too seriously, we are actually raising all sorts of mental barriers. We are on full alert for anything that could breach our self-created veneer of professionalism-without-personality.

Unfortunately, among the barbarians thwarted at the moat are those fleeting creative notions and ideas.

Once we lower the draw-bridge and allow ourselves to be less serious, the alert comes to an end. We are telling our brain that it's ok to let things through the barriers. When we then engage with our teams in this new, lighter fashion, it's also likely that laughter will ensue at some point. We will then be engaged, we will feel good and we stand a good chance of having a creative idea slip past the 'stupid' barrier.

In my previous role directing the global logistics of a large international steel company, I looked forward to my end-of-week managers meeting. While there was always some news to be shared with everyone, its secondary purpose was to allow for venting and catching up with one another, personally. It usually wasn't very long before we were all laughing heartily at something or other. When the laughter subsided, we would be able to look at the remaining pressing issues in a much lighter frame of mind.

We weren't always successful at finding creative solutions during those meetings, but somehow, over the weekend, new ideas would suddenly come to light. We were then able to spend the following week considering and trying out the new ideas. Sometimes these attempts proved good comedic fodder for the following week's meetings.

While some might argue that it was the relaxing nature of the upcoming week-end that boosted creativity, I would argue otherwise based on the lack of ideas prior to these meetings. After all, the weekends were there every week prior to my meetings so why weren't ideas flowing then? I firmly believe that the lighter meetings served as a brain primer, setting the stage for creative ideas to flow more freely.

Key Takeaways:
1) We can be serious about our responsibilities without necessarily taking ourselves so seriously.
2) Laughter is a key component to team engagement and team creativity.

PRINCIPLE 2
SEPARATE IDEA GENERATION FROM IDEA EVALUATION

This next principle is perhaps one of the more difficult steps to execute. The biggest barrier to achieving this principle is our own subconscious. When we first asked for as many brick uses as possible without a minimum or a time limit, we only received a relative few suggestions. Our own brains ignored this creative concept and pre-selected for us only those ideas that it deemed 'not-stupid', practical, realistic, legal, ethical, and so on. The result was only a few time-worn and time-tested (conventional) uses.

We also saw this concept rear its ugly head in my example of the Six Sigma Green Belt training exercise (coming up with areas in which the company is excelling and those in which it needs improvement). In that case, one participant's subconscious mind did not eliminate their non-conventional thought, leaving it, instead, to an executive (who did not follow directions, nor play well) to discard it.

The result reinforced the notion that the subconscious actually does us a favor by eliminating the non-conventional for us. For our daily routine and related tasks, we expect not to be bombarded by myriad ideas and thoughts floating in our brain. After all, we need to focus on the task at hand to complete it successfully . Thus, the 'stupid' filter is a necessary and desirable thing to have in order to function effectively on a daily basis. Unfortunately, this necessity also wreaks havoc with our creative abilities.

As a professional general aviation pilot, I frequently undergo recurrent training and frequently look to expand my skills through lessons learned in other forms of flying. While I don't expect to pursue aerobatic flying (upon wife-inflicted pain of death), the lessons learned from its training are applicable in everyday flights. As part of this type of expanded training, I recently undertook 'upset recovery' training. For those readers who are not pilots, this is recovery from flight that is outside of the normal flying attitude (inverted flight, for example). This training took place in a full-motion simulator that replicated not only the motion of the plane but also the actual gravitational (G) forces present in recovering from upset flight. One of the key takeaways (besides the "don't-try-this-one-at-home") is that multi-tasking is mostly mythical.

While most of us have the ability to walk down the street and chew bubble gum at the same time without requiring a helmet or an insurance rider, we cannot focus simultaneously on more than one task. When we focus on one task, our situational awareness outside of that task diminishes rapidly.

A perfect example of the fallacy of multi-tasking is texting while driving. The attention required when texting greatly and rapidly decreases the outside awareness necessary to drive safely. If nothing changes suddenly during this time, everything is fine. But if something, even something relatively small, changes while we are texting and driving, we are unable to perceive it or the threat it may present. The result is frequently a car accident. The only way around this is through extremely rapid scanning without any fixation and this tactic doesn't work well (if at all) in the congested world of driving. Similar arguments have been made for any type of distracted driving, whether it is mobile phone usage, eating or drinking. We need to stay consciously focused and we rely on our subconscious to filter out everything other than what those sensory inputs deem essential.

While the subconscious and its filters perform admirably when confronted with certain tasks, it doesn't switch off, on-command, when we really don't want the filter applied (for example, when generating new ideas). By doing this 'good job' for us, it prevents us from moving forward, we cannot innovate and we certainly can't address properly the problems and issues confronting us. So for creativity, is it really doing such a 'good job'?

Since we can't arbitrarily turn off the subconscious, the best we can do is to fool it by removing common barrier inputs. With the brick exercise, we fooled it by imposing a time limit and a quantity minimum. This, in essence, told the subconscious that the 'stupid' barrier had been removed and that it was alright just to spit out any idea that came to mind, even those only remotely relevant (if at all), regardless of applicability. The brain was too busy with this task to judge any idea. In its failure to multitask, 50-plus ideas for usage were generated. Even if, ultimately, 70% of these ideas are too far-fetched to be used, that next great idea is much more likely to emanate from the remaining ones.

A quick bit of math will help better illustrate this concept in action.

We typically have 20 people in each of our workshops so, by mathematical extension: 20 people times 50 brick usage ideas equals 1000 total ideas minus 60% duplication equals 400 remaining ideas minus 70% impracticality equals 120 remaining ideas. If I were a brick manufacturer or marketer, I might be interested in those 120 ideas. Imagine this were an electronic item or medicine, what is the value of those 120 ideas in whole or in part?

Now, if we just left it with the subconscious not fooled, the math might look like this: 20 people times 6 (average number generated per person) brick ideas equals 120 ideas, minus 90% duplication (the duplication factor is higher since there are limited conventional brick uses) equals 12 ideas, minus a variable impracticality percentage equals 5-10 remaining ideas. If you were this same marketer, which set of ideas would be likely to generate greater interest?

Of course, most meetings held to stimulate idea generation don't involve the common brick. These meetings, frequently called brainstorming sessions, are designed to allow for discovery of creative and innovative solutions to real problems and issues. Unfortunately, brainstorming, besides the subconscious barrier, also has the active 'dominator barrier' (by which I mean that those speaking the loudest, frequently over others, are often the most senior participants). Even in meetings in which everybody is working well together, many people just don't want to risk looking stupid; some people are uncomfortable offering up ideas publicly and many people are difficult to actively engage in this process.

The result is a significant number of non-communicated and unrealized ideas. One of these ideas just might be the impetus that solves the problem or propels the company forward, but sadly, it is unlikely ever to be realized. The challenge is getting these ideas communicated so they stand the chance of being realized and utilized.

For my Culture of Innovation workshops, I ideally like to work with a group of 20-25 people (which is typically larger than a normal corporate brainstorming group). But even if there are fewer people, I will still attempt a brainstorming session. I tend to solicit from the attendees a common business issue, not too specific but also not too broad. For example, a good (not-too-specific) common business issue is how to market a service/product more effectively. By comparison an example of a theme that is too broad is "we need more sales".

This brainstorming session will last, by design, for approximately nine minutes. Out of this nine-minute session, we'll usually receive ten ideas in the first few minutes and perhaps another few over the remaining time. Most of these ideas will be offered by the same three or four people. Others will raise their hands but then lower them after hearing another's idea. At the end, we'll have 15 ideas or so. Some of these ideas will be rough duplicates, even though they might have been worded slightly differently.

After the brainstorming session is complete, we'll engage in a different idea generation method using the very same problem. However, this time I'll hand out a pad of regular-sized lined paper to each attendee. I will then instruct them, in a timed three-minute period, to write down three-to-five ideas to solve the problem without using any of the previously stated ideas. For the exercise, we'll pretend that all of those ideas have been tried without resolving the issue and cannot be written down now.

At the end of the three minutes, I will collect all the papers, mix them up (ensuring that no one receives their previously submitted answers) and redistribute them face down. We will then repeat the three minutes and I'll advise everyone to read the written ideas and use them to generate another three-to-five ideas. We will then repeat this a third time, for a total of nine minutes of idea-generation time.

The results are fantastic, whether we have everyone engaged individually or in small groups. Nobody has a difficulty generating 15 ideas (five ideas times three iterations). Everyone is engaged and has the full freedom and security to write down any idea that pops in their heads. Mathematically, 20 people times 15 ideas equals 300 ideas to solve a common business issue in nine minutes!

If we cared to evaluate the quality of those ideas: 300 ideas minus 40% duplication equals 180 ideas, minus 70% impracticality (conservative estimate) equals 54 ideas. In nine minutes, without anyone being alienated and with everyone fully engaged, we generated 54 practical ideas to solve this common business problem. Many times, the impracticality percentage will be lower than 70%, creating even more practical ideas to be considered.

This alternate method is referred to as brain-writing and is being implemented more frequently as companies seek out progressive methods for idea generation. However, for it to work properly in a corporate setting, use of a skilled and unbiased moderator is required. In fact, in a recent paper in *Harvard Business Review*, a study found that virtual brainstorming (or brain-writing) can enhance creativity by nearly 50% of a standard deviation. In layman's terms, this means that 70% of participants in a typical brainstorming session will perform worse (and have fewer good ideas) than in a virtual brainstorming or brain-writing session (Chamorro-Permuzic, Thomas, *Harvard Business Review*, April 2, 2015).

Perhaps the biggest barrier to successful brainstorming or brain-writing is use of this skilled and unbiased moderator. Without a moderator, potentially productive meetings quickly transform from idea generation to idea judgment. The result is a premature end to active engagement of everyone involved and the resulting missed impactful ideas.

If you would like to see the perils of brainstorming in action, quietly observe your next company/team brainstorming session. If I were a gambling person (which, of course, I still am), I would bet strongly that, with the very first idea presented, there will be immediate comments regarding its viability or practicality. And once someone has had their idea publicly attacked, this person (and any other participant that observes this public flogging) will offer up very few further ideas, if any at all, for fear of suffering the same fate. I have, to date, never observed a brainstorming session (without the skilled moderator) that didn't quickly descend into the judgment phase. This is why there is a critical need for a skilled moderator who can quickly, and diplomatically, address any attacks or other judging comments during the session.

In fact, when I am the designated moderator, whether in our workshops or with clients, I assume the role of a football referee (sometimes complete with the cap, whistle and yellow penalty flags). If I overhear anyone starting to judge an idea during the idea-generation phase, I will quickly intervene to short-circuit the judging. As anyone in my workshops can attest, nothing grabs everyone's attention as quickly as a shrill whistle and tracking the arc of the thrown penalty flag. What is the infraction? Delay of idea – five yards and repeat of process. Is this a bit much? Yes, but it guarantees others stop judging and it shows everyone that all ideas will be protected regardless of stature, practicality or realism.

> Frequently, the difficulty in generating corporate ideas is in deciding who is invited to the party in the first place.

But there are other barriers to successful corporate idea generation efforts. Frequently, the difficulty in generating corporate ideas is in deciding who is invited to the party in the first place. In many companies, the invited list is only certain people at a certain managerial level or above. The thought process is that the company cannot trust its future to just anybody. Of course, we all should know that hierarchical level is not indicative of quality or quantity of ideas. In fact, a vice president doesn't have a monopoly on great ideas any more than the shipping clerk or the machine operator. Unfortunately, many companies have difficulty reconciling what they should know (and perhaps even subconsciously acknowledge) with what they put and/or are willing to put into action.

The common way of addressing this is the proverbial suggestion box or suggestion email address, where any and all ideas are allegedly welcome. I can definitively state, based on experience, observation and interviews, that this method is less than effective (admit it; you rolled your eyes when you read "suggestion box"). While many reasons for this abound, the likely culprit is simple lack of trust.

Without trust, there is no teamwork, engagement or buy-in. Unless that suggestion box is attached to a visible and viable idea-generation system, it quickly becomes a standing joke. If ideas submitted via this method are not acknowledged, how does anyone know that they are being considered? If some of these ideas are not implemented, does anyone think their ideas really matter? How likely will it be that this method will result in a consistently full pipeline of ideas? All of this legitimate questioning leads to an erosion of trust with idea generation being the first victim.

Additionally, the person who has come up with the idea is likely to be proud of their idea. There is pride of ownership, and if someone contributes, they expect acknowledgment should the idea be used in some fashion. This is an investment and the idea contributor expects a personal return on investment (PROI). The return doesn't have to be financial, but there must be some sort of meaningful recognition. Sadly, many companies do not have, nor are they willing to employ, such mechanisms. We'll talk more about PROI and its role in successful change management later in the book, but for now, can we agree to banish the standard suggestion box and either create a more dynamic suggestion mechanism and/or employ a skilled moderator instead?

This mechanism/moderator should solicit feedback and ideas from everyone in the company, regardless of level, position or stature. This should be employed regardless of whether the issue affects everyone or just a division or department. Email or intranet is the most common idea-delivery method and allows for ease of collection and aggregation.

Another practical way is through the use of a third-party internet portal. These third-party sites assume the role of the unbiased moderator and are able to both protect the anonymity of the idea source (unless their idea is selected for further consideration) and aggregate the ideas for consideration by an idea selection group.

Finally, there is the demonstrated 'Kickboxing method', so ably employed by Adobe Systems. The Kickbox is a small red box containing everything anyone would need to originate, build and test innovations. Inspired by Mark Randall, vice president of creativity for Adobe as a way to place multiple bets on new ideas, the Kickbox is available to anyone who requests it and cannot be vetoed by any manager. Inside the Kickbox are instructions, sticky note pads, notebooks, a coffee shop gift card, a bar of chocolate and a $1,000 prepaid credit card, which can be used without pre-approval or expense reporting. The Kickbox relies on a six-step litmus test that has the idea socialized in larger groups before the final step of senior management approval.

Results so far have been a handful of ideas that Adobe is currently pursuing but, even more importantly, a renewed enthusiasm and engagement as well as the creation of a wide-open idea pipeline without the fear of bias or pre-judging. (*Sources:*Burkus, D, Inside Adobe's Innovation Kit, *Harvard Business Review*, February 23, 2015; *Raymundo, Oscar,* How to Build a Secret Army of Innovators, *Inc.com, December12, 2014*)

Whether this method of generation is sustainable, or even replicable, is a matter of debate, as ultimately an organization's ability to generate ideas is bound by its innovation culture (or lack of it). However, just the presence of an innovative idea to generate other innovative ideas, raises the conversation volume and will undoubtedly inspire further idea-generation strategies, tactics and tools.

When practical, the invited list of brainstorming attendees should be as broad as is workable. The narrower the list, the less varied and diverse the idea-generation pool becomes. While I strongly advocate for larger groups being involved, I have seen positive results in groups of as few as ten people, provided that there is role and departmental diversity. But even with these 'good' results from the smaller group, I would maintain that more people would result in more ideas. Simply put, the larger the idea pool, the greater the likelihood of finding actionable and implementable ideas.

There should be absolutely no adverse consequence or recourse for any responsibly communicated idea, regardless of its impracticality or realism. There should also be a recognition and incentive mechanism for any idea used in whole, or in part, to encourage others to contribute their ideas in the next idea generation cycle. Finally, when presenting these ideas for evaluation, any and all identifying information should be removed so that the ideas are being evaluated purely on merit without any bias towards (or against) the originator.

This method has been proven to work, and if conducted correctly, leads to some incredible ideas. Of course, the process cannot work if we are judging ideas, either subconsciously or overtly, as the ideas are being generated. Likewise, there should be no artificial barriers or 'boxes' imposed.

I, like many other people, cringe at the overused and meaningless statement "think outside the box". I also look with curiosity at others who espouse thinking "inside the box". All of this focus on 'the box' or pre-set parameters or rules is injurious to the creative process. There is a time for critical evaluation of ideas and methods to ensure bias plays a minor, if any, role; it's just not now, during the idea generation phase.

There should be absolutely no boxes at all during the idea generation phase. No parameters, no rules. The only concept should be total freedom to capture whatever fleeting notion pops up. I refer to this as the "why the hell not?" concept of creativity. If we continuously ask ourselves this question (without

Without trust, there is no teamwork, engagement or buy-in.

answering it), there is no limit to our potential discoveries during the idea-generation phase.

Of course, many people will argue reasonably that all thinking should be 'inside the box' and that the best ideas don't start with a blank canvas. In fact, they will quote recognized studies that show this to be true. Furthermore, they will argue that since 'the box' is so frequently misrepresented, the better method is to explore the existing parameters fully, or even expand the box.

So who's right and which way should we go?

Actually, we're both right, despite the apparent contradictory nature of our beliefs. As I stated earlier, clear definition of the problem is critical to generating ideas that might solve it. As a Lean Six Sigma Black Belt, I certainly wouldn't trivialize the concept of 'Define' and its requirements for a clear charter.

So yes, ideation should start with the clear definition (or parameter, or 'box') of the problem, but that's where the definition should stop. In fact, the whole concept of cross-functional teams relies on the notion that different experiences and perspectives will ultimately lead to a more productive team.

In a recent conversation with Mark Keller, president of Fontaine Engineered Products, a Berkshire Hathaway Company, the importance of cross-functional (meaning individuals from different sections and of different ranks) teams during the innovation process, was stressed. At Fontaine, the process started with cross-functional group meetings, whose participants were tasked with originating ideas to solve complex problems requiring exploration. The next step included a different cross-functional team comprising research and development (R&D), marketing, sales, manufacturing and a member of the executive team to carry out a preliminary study including markets, costs and goals, all with the goal of gaining a complete understanding of the likely markets. Next steps included higher-level strategic review, timetable and required resource generation followed by a product development process.

Mark further stressed that the understanding from senior executives that "sometimes failure is part of being a success" was a required component in the team's overall innovative success. In essence, the company allows people to fail (through innovative pursuit) without fear of being at risk. Naturally, with failure comes financial cost and more importantly, discouragement, as everyone wishes to

> In fact, the whole concept of cross-functional teams relies on the notion that different experiences and perspectives will ultimately lead to a more productive team.

succeed, but senior leadership continues to encourage innovation with an eye to being more competitive, improving safety and/or reducing costs. These understandings lead to overall faith and trust in senior management with other change initiatives and help bring everyone on board.

Naturally, how a company embarks on both change and innovation is reflective of its overall culture, which in this case is reflective of the successful culture of Warren Buffet and Berkshire Hathaway.

Should it be any different with ideation? Why should we artificially limit the horizons of thought and notion? If an idea generated is truly impractical or impossible, based on established and infallible criteria, it should be set aside later in the process (during the idea judgment phase). Why shouldn't we actively encourage people to use their experiences, backgrounds and imagination to suggest any way of solving the problem? What would we lose by allowing this? Better yet, what could we ultimately gain? Why the hell not?

The key takeaways: *When generating ideas, we must:*
1) suspend judgment, both subconsciously and consciously
2) remove the 'stupid' barrier
3) generate ideas using a clearly defined problem/issue but then solve it without artificial limits, boundaries, rules or 'boxes'

PRINCIPLE 3
ALWAYS TEST
ASSUMPTIONS

However, even with the directive of no rules, no limits, no parameters and so on, we are still faced with another significant internal barrier. If we revisit our brick exercise, why did we initially only unearth six or seven uses and then later 'discover' 50 or more?

The answer lies within our own assumptive thought processes. We assumed that the brick could only be used conventionally, as we commonly see it used or as society (however we define this) expects us to use it.

Of course, we are all familiar with the concept that the word 'assume' is really a partial acronym, ASS + U + ME. In other words, when we assume, we make fools out of everyone involved, ourselves included. Now, considering we are internally wired not to do anything that makes us look stupid, why are we naturally inclined to assume?

Before we answer, let's clarify the difference between absolute knowledge and assumed knowledge. Absolute knowledge is objective fact, unsullied by opinion or conjecture. When we say that the sun rises in the east and sets in the west, it is absolute and not assumptive. But if last night, we saw a forecast that it would be rainy tomorrow and we left our house with all our raingear without checking the forecast again prior to leaving, that would be assumptive. We have made an assumption based on an advance forecast (essentially an educated guess) that it would be rainy. We might be right, but it's also possible that the weather front stalls and/or the clouds dissipate overnight and there is no need for the raingear.

Assumption is highly prevalent in our everyday lives. We so frequently and constantly confuse opinion for fact that what is really an absolute becomes muddled in what we think are absolutes. Politicians and talk show commentators thrive on this very notion.

Consider the politician who does something wrong, be it an extra-marital affair, ill-advised comment, tax fraud, controversial tweet and so on. After the requisite adamant denials and self-propelled quests to uncover the truth, an apology is usually forthcoming.

The apology almost always follows the same script: "I apologize if anyone was offended by my comments/actions". We, the public and the frequent patrons of the short-attention-span theatre, quickly *assume* that an apology has been issued and we go about our business. We may even debate whether or not the apology was sincere or just sincerely self-serving, but somehow always miss the point. The politician never actually apologized or showed any real remorse (usually a prerequisite for a real apology). The politician apologized for someone else being offended, but not for the actual offensive action. We just assumed that he had apologized.

Reality television is yet another example of assumptive power. We believe that what we are seeing from the contestants is reflective of their true selves. We watch and come to love or hate a particular contestant based on their television persona. We get sucked into this under the premise that it's real (after all, it is called reality television). We assume that it must be true and that person we have grown to dislike must really be a jerk and we hope that they get eliminated soon. Even if we disregard the fact that what we see is what the producers want us to see and is likely not the real persona, our assumption is based on a snippet of footage, here or there. We don't really know the person or their history, only what we perceive, based on extremely limited observation.

When we say that perception is 90% of reality, we are actually screaming that we are categorical and prolific assumers. We assume that even a limited interaction with a person is a valid substitute for discovering what the person truly represents. Maybe we'll make some casual inquiries, but even if those inquiries contrast with our perception, we'll still give outsized credence to our own perceptions and assumptions.

The point is that we need to be aware of just how powerful and controlling our assumptive subconscious and conscious selves truly are.

On the other hand, assumption might not always be a bad thing. Someone who always gives people the benefit of the doubt is usually looked upon favorably, even though the assumption of positive action might be misplaced. In fact, the US criminal court system is based on this benefit of the doubt. The prevailing instruction given to juries in a criminal case is that a guilty verdict cannot be reached until the evidence proves guilt beyond reasonable doubt. There is an overpowering presumption of innocence until the evidence proves otherwise.

For the sake of creativity and the overall creative process, assumptions must always be tested and retested. There are many ways to test assumptions, with two of the best ways being the 5-Why and Intelligent Fast Failure (IFF) methods. While both of these methods are integral to successful change management, they are also key tools in combating our natural inclination to assume.

The 5-Why method is akin to resurrecting our inner- and over-inquisitive three-year-old selves. We can imagine the ensuing inner conversation when confronted with our brick:

Inner child (IC): "What is that?"
Adult self (AS): "It's a brick, which is used for building things."
IC: "Why?"
AS: "Because it's strong and sturdy."
IC: "Why?"
AS: "Because it's made out of compressed sand and gravel."
IC: "Why?"
AS: "Because they allow for inexpensive formation."
IC: "Why?"
AS: "Because they are in abundant and easy supply."
IC: "Why?"
AS: "Because it's everywhere."

And so on. The point is that this inner conversation occurs in milliseconds. The subconscious has already assumed that the primary use for this brick is to build things and the remaining inner conversation is designed to justify this assumption. This concept of post-action rationalization is prevalent in psychological

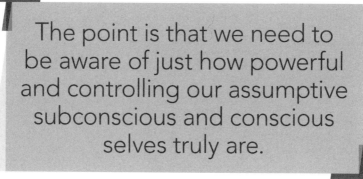

The point is that we need to be aware of just how powerful and controlling our assumptive subconscious and conscious selves truly are.

studies and thought. We will frequently take actions without any recognizable active conscious thought (albeit, the subconscious never stops working) and then only afterwards, conjure up a reason for why the action taken was appropriate.

For our purposes, it's only after we concluded that the brick is intended for building that we started to think of the appropriateness of our conclusion – all of this rapidly happening in our subconscious.

Now, what if we made a conscious decision to question the assumption that the brick's primary purpose is to build things? When we first ask why, we are also acknowledging that there may be other uses for this brick aside from its initially assumed use. In other words, at the end, the "why?" is now followed by a "why not?" (or as I prefer, a "why the hell not?").

Why is the brick used for building purposes instead of as a projectile? Why can't we use this brick as a projectile? And what if we were to grind up this brick and use the dust to increase traction in paint? Why not? What if we could find some medicinal use for this dust? Why not? What if we could create a light-weight version of this brick and use it for a spaceship? Why not? What if we could create a brick made of foam instead of sand and gravel so we could throw it at things and release stress, without damaging anything? Why not? The iterations are infinite and so are the possibilities, once we consciously challenge and test assumptions.

One of our most popular workshop exercises, 'I Scream for Ice Cream', specifically illustrates both testing assumptions and Intelligent Fast Failure. This exercise is inspired by the 'popsicle sticks' activity given by Dr Jack Matson, Emeritus professor of environmental engineering at Penn State University, a recognized leader in practical innovation as well as innovation theory and author of *Innovate or Die, (Paradigm Press, 1996)*.

Our exercise is specifically designed so that every table has only three, four or five people around it. Each group is given 30 enhanced Popsicle® (or ice cream) sticks. These sticks, sometimes referred to as smart sticks, have notches and grooves on their sides to allow for the possibility of linking one or more of them together. The challenge is to build the tallest structure in a timed period of 25 minutes. No other instruction or direction is given. And then we start the clock...

While no limits or rules have been communicated, it's always quite interesting to see which groups assume that they can't use tape, glue or staples (all hidden in plain sight around the room) and struggle to agree on a building process which might work and which groups (also making an assumption) believe that, if it isn't expressly forbidden, it's allowed. Another assumption is that this is a win-lose exercise when, in reality, there are no winners or losers. The entire purpose of the exercise is to illustrate the power of assumptive thought and Intelligent Fast Failure.

For the sake
of creativity
and the overall
creative process,
assumptions must
always be tested
and retested.

The 25 minutes passes in a relative heartbeat and with the proverbial buzzer, the exercise is concluded. Without fail, the groups that spent considerable time planning and then executing were less successful than those that continuously tinkered and experimented with different assembly methods. This, in essence, is Intelligent Fast Failure in action. By engaging in multiple limited and quick experiments in the construction of the structures, the participants were quickly able to determine what would and wouldn't work. This ongoing process of limited experimentation and subsequent determination allowed for a more feasible and stronger final structure design.

While in-depth planning is critical to any initiative, it must be accompanied with simultaneous limited experimentation. By starting this limited experimentation earlier in the process, failures will undoubtedly be encountered and lessons will be learned. These lessons can then be applied to further experimentation and will ultimately lead to a stronger and more resilient final result.

The key is to allow for this limited experimentation in a controlled fashion, so that the failures can have distinct and recognizable causes. In the stick exercise, when people immediately started experimenting with assembly, they discovered rather quickly which methods worked, which ones worked better and which ones were doomed to fail. Lessons learned from these quick failures allowed greater focus on other experimental methods, with the ultimate result being a taller structure.

Other things we have observed after conducting this exercise: Some groups are incredibly interpretive with the challenge of 'tallest structure'. There are groups that build a structure that isn't tall from the ground up, but rather in length or width. Others will place a stick or two on a picture frame hanging in the room or on an otherwise tall object in the room. We've even had some groups put the sticks on the roof or the highest floor of the building. Other groups will find a picture of a tall building and put a stick or two on the picture. Who's to say that a stick on a picture of the Empire State Building isn't now the tallest stick structure? Finally, there were groups that both assembled a conventionally defined tall structure and interpreted the challenge in other, more creative, ways (for example, by placing the structure on top of a chair or cases or whatever else they could find to place it on).

There is another way to highlight the necessity of integrating Intelligent Fast Failure into the idea generation and creative process phases. Imagine that you and three friends are taking a plane trip across rugged, mountainous terrain. Suddenly, the plane (piloted by one of your friends) has a mechanical failure and is forced to make an emergency landing in a large forest clearing. The plane lands without incident, but after quickly surveying the situation, you realize your group is ill prepared for this new reality. You surmise that you are in some sort of canyon and recall, during the descent, seeing some roads in the general vicinity, but in the ruckus of the emergency landing don't recall their relative direction. You have enough food and water for two days. How will your group best determine its exit route before running out of provisions?

For the sake of this exercise, we will establish some parameters.

Parameter 1: The exit route is in a cardinal direction (due north, east, west or south) rather than some variant (such as northwest, southeast) and is no more than half a day's walk away

Parameter 2: All other possible variables (weather, individual walking speed, mental condition and so on) are inherently accounted for and do not impact the overall probability of success

Parameter 3: Since no one is to be left behind, everyone must return to the clearing at the end of each day, even if they have discovered the exit route (unless everyone is on the exit route)

Parameter 4: If the group makes it to the outside road, it will quickly be discovered and rescued

If the entire group proceeds in one cardinal direction at a time, the chance of finding the exit route is 25% (one in four) the first day and only 33% (one in three) the second day (since one route was eliminated on day one, the odds lowered to one in three on day two.) Those are not great survival odds. If however, the group splits into two, then the odds are 50% on day one (two out of four). Day two's chances are 100% for one group and 0% for the other group (or 50% if everyone proceeds on one of the two remaining routes). Thus, on either day, the entire group's survival relies on little more than a coin flip determining the direction. On day two, one group of two will find a way out of the canyon, while the other group of two won't, since they will, by chance, be travelling on the wrong route. If everyone returns at the end of the day, all will know the survival route but then also be out of time.

Alternatively, on day two, the entire group of four could choose to go in one of the remaining two directions but again their survival chances are just 50% as they have a one in two probability of picking the correct remaining direction. Once again, the group's survival hinges on nothing more than a coin flip.

However, there is a method that guarantees a 100% success rate (for the entire group) in finding the exit route. If, on day one, each member of the group sets out in a different cardinal direction and returns by nightfall to the clearing, then the exit route will be discovered. On day two, the entire group can exit the canyon using the route successfully discovered the previous day.

The successful version of the canyon exercise is essentially four experiments conducted simultaneously. Each group member's journey to discovering the exit route is its own experiment. Individually, the failure rate was 75% with a success rate of 25% (one out of four), but using the combined knowledge from the three failed experiments (the three routes that didn't lead to the canyon exit), the success rate jumps to 100% (on day two). Intelligent Fast Failure operates using a similar premise, without necessarily the life and death outcome.

In essence, we have failed our way to success. But do we actually need to fail to succeed? And is failure critical to the creative process?

If we posit that both failure and success are relative terms, then these failures (on day one) were not conventionally defined failures, rather a means to an end. Therefore, if we define success as survival of the entire group, guaranteed success relied on the multiple individual failures.

Taken further, progressive organizations understand that many initiatives will not achieve their initial success criteria. However, they continue to encourage and fund these and other initiatives because of what is learned from the experiences. And from this learning, new and better ideas will emerge, ultimately leading to breakthroughs and achievable, conventionally defined successes. Thus, people on the initiative teams (who failed) become in high demand for other roles and other initiative teams. The prevailing thought is, "What have we learned and how can we use this knowledge?"

Intelligent Fast Failure (shortened to IFF below) is, by definition, non-linear and non-sequential (at least not in the conventional thinking). This makes it an optimal tool for several different components of the creative process, especially when we

> Once we allow ourselves the ability to have initiative failure without adverse consequence or reaction, we actually open the subconscious doorway even further.

wish to test assumptions. By design, IFF states that one plus one doesn't necessarily equal two. Furthermore, IFF means that the number three doesn't necessarily follow the number two, which in turn doesn't necessarily follow the number one.

The creative process relies on our more conceptual definition of failure (means to an end) to refine the idea and to allow for emergence of descendant ideas. In fact, when we later discuss idea judgment, this concept will become more apparent. Once we allow ourselves the ability to have initiative failure without adverse consequence or reaction, we actually open the subconscious doorway even further.

Consider a construction project timeline as a real-world example of non-linear and non-sequential actions. The prevailing assumption should be that each part of the construction relies on the preceding completion of the previous step. In other words, step two cannot commence until step one is completed. While it is certainly true that some steps do require preceding steps to be completed, a construction timeline would be extended significantly if all steps proceeded sequentially. We know that many different steps are being performed simultaneously. For instance, while wood framing is being built on one level, the electricians might already be working somewhere else, the plumbers working in a different location and concrete work might be taking place in a third location.

Similarly, with the creative process (which is almost always multi-tasked and multi-faceted), we are frequently able to think of diverse and disparate thoughts and ideas that might not fit in a linear fashion. If we simply eliminate these notions now because of the apparent disorder, we will lose the opportunity later to have it 'make sense'. But if we record them and continue forward, we can continue to think and ideate creatively. At some point, a working order (rhyme and reason) will emerge, with the result being something new (in other words, innovative).

While one can make an argument that there is still a step one, in that there has to be a beginning, I would argue that there can be, and are, many beginning steps (step ones) in most efficient construction projects. Why should 'construction' of ideas be any different? Why should we assume anything when thinking of ways to be better, to be more profitable and more innovative?

The English language provides us with even more ways to test assumptions. While synonyms can have similar or identical meanings, there can be a world of difference in perception (assumptive thought). A perfect example is the comparison between the words 'stubborn' and 'tenacious'. They both mean approximately the same thing; sticking with something, a quality of perseverance in an opinion or action.

So why is it that if you call someone 'stubborn', it is usually taken to be derogatory or critical, while calling someone 'tenacious' is usually a compliment, a virtuous quality? Can someone be stubbornly good or tenaciously bad?

They essentially mean the same thing, but create almost opposite perceptions. Technically, they can and should be interchanged freely, but we are conditioned, based on assumptions, to consider them dissimilar. As an experiment (you can try this at home), substitute 'tenacious' when you normally would use 'stubborn' and vice versa. Note the reactions, and of course, those that might correct you (even though your usage is both technically and grammatically correct). When we assume or rely on assumptions, we close ourselves off to other possibilities. And when we close ourselves off to these possibilities, we also close ourselves off to being creative. Aren't some people so tenacious?

In our ice cream stick exercise, we never communicated a rule stating that a group couldn't creatively interpret 'tall' as they wished. Some groups however, assumed they couldn't. We never communicated any rule preventing the use of glue, tape or staples. However, some groups assumed they couldn't use them. If you must assume (in the absence of any rule or guidance), assume that you can do something rather than you can't. Assume that it is possible, rather than impossible.

These same groups would initially protest that the interpretive groups 'cheated' and that the groups that used tape or glue also 'cheated'. But it's only cheating if there is an absolute rule. It's not cheating if one group makes one assumption and the others make a different one. In other words, where there isn't a rule, it's not possible to cheat.

And even if we did conclude there was 'cheating', why is it a bad thing if the only thing 'cheated' or 'fooled' was our own subconscious inclination to assume. In fact, I would strongly defend this 'cheating' as a method of unlocking our innate creative and innovative selves.

Key takeaways:
1) *By suspending assumptive thought and not assuming anything, we open the door for creative thought.*
2) *We can also actively test assumptions using 5-Why and Intelligent Fast Failure.*
3) *Failure is but a means to an end and is thus a critical component of the creative process.*
4) *Where there is no rule, there is no cheating. We should assume that something is possible rather than impossible.*

PRINCIPLE 4
AVOID PATTERNED
THINKING

It's not our fault that we are wired to assume. We are trained this way even from a very early age. My youngest daughter is 23 months old and many of her toys are designed to teach patterned thought. There is the toy that has a plastic pole, which starts off thick and thins out towards the top. This toy has six different-colored plastic rings with varying center-hole diameters. The goal is to place the widest diameter ring on the bottom and build the rings up to the top, matching each ring with the pole width and center-hole diameter. Other toys have boxes with different shapes cut out of the sides and the goal is to place the plastic shape cutouts in the proper shape holes.

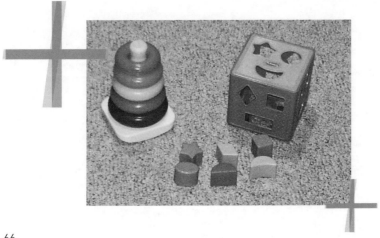

These toys are essential to build cognitive ability but they also teach patterned thought. There can only be one proper solution and the child, through experimentation, discovers and learns the right one.

Patterned thought is further reinforced in children's television shows. Even something like Mickey Mouse Clubhouse® teaches that certain objects do certain things while other items do not accomplish the set task. Sesame Street® has a long-running feature called, *One of these things doesn't belong*, the idea being to find the one item that is least like the others. In early math, we are taught patterns in numbers and orders. All of this is essential and necessary, but it reinforces patterned thinking. Furthermore, in some ways, even the creative side of children's education also reinforces patterned thinking.

Consider an arts and crafts project to make a construction-paper turkey for Thanksgiving. The truly creative way would be either to a) show a picture of a turkey to the class or b) show a completed construction paper turkey to the class and then allow everyone to construct their turkey as they imagine it. Undoubtedly, the results will bear out their creative efforts.

Instead, a *pattern* of a turkey is shown by the teacher along with specific directions in assembling the disparate parts. The only creative discretion might be the colors of the construction paper used and any personal message written by the child. The result is that there is virtually no diversity in how the turkeys look. There may be some circles and shapes cut slightly differently depending on how well the child cuts the traced pattern, but overall they are all the same and follow the same pattern. While it is still a worthwhile activity (I always enjoyed the diversion), I doubt it could truly be called a creative exercise.

The issue with patterned thinking is that it diminishes our ability to think creatively and to innovate. We are very reluctant to tamper with the established order of things and we are quick to eliminate from consideration those things that don't fall within our regular patterns. This is why we have such difficulty making changes in our own lives and in the corporate world. We crave stability and our routines and patterns provide this comfort for us. All is fine and good until the need arises to find a new way and change. This comfort-craving inertia is a powerful force requiring very different thinking and methods to breakthrough.

As further proof, try this exercise out with one or more colleagues. Have the colleague(s) quickly repeat the word "joke" five times. When he finishes,

> How well and how confidently we propel ourselves outside our comfort zones is critical to the success of the initiative and perhaps the enterprise as a whole.

immediately ask him what the white part of egg is called. The immediate response will most likely be "yolk". It is only after more thought is applied, that the realization sets in that 'yolk' is actually the yellow part of the egg and not the white part (which is actually called albumen). We have been trained using rhyming as a pattern. Thus, the immediate inclination to say "yolk" is because it rhymes with "joke". Patterns aren't necessarily bad things, and in fact are critical to decision making, but they do interfere with creative thought and with unbridled idea generation.

The ability to break out of routines and patterns is also a critical component in public speaking and with executive communications as a whole. Typically, this is referred to as "leaving your comfort zone". We all have things about which we are comfortable and confident speaking, although perhaps not publicly. Unfortunately, there are times when the communication required falls well outside this zone.

Exiting the comfort zone will typically take place when delivering bad news (for example, downsizing, plant closings, letting an employee go). It will also be necessary in high-stress situations. These are the very same situations that require creative and innovative thought (and of course, empathy) to alleviate the causes and influencers of this stress. How well and how confidently we propel ourselves outside our comfort zones is critical to the success of the initiative and perhaps the enterprise as a whole.

One of the first courses in my MBA program was executive communications. Of course, the old adage that people are more afraid of public speaking than death was the major barrier the course sought to overcome. One of the first tasks involved a poem by Lewis Carroll, of *Alice in Wonderland* fame, called *Jabberwocky* (*Through the Looking-Glass and What Alice Found There*, 1872).

> `Twas brillig, and the slithy toves
> Did gyre and gimble in the wabe:
> All mimsy were the borogoves,
> And the mome raths outgrabe.
>
> "Beware the Jabberwock, my son!
> The jaws that bite, the claws that catch!
> Beware the Jubjub bird, and shun
> The frumious Bandersnatch!"
>
> He took his vorpal sword in hand:
> Long time the manxome foe he sought --
> So rested he by the Tumtum tree,
> And stood awhile in thought.
>
> And, as in uffish thought he stood,
> The Jabberwock, with eyes of flame,
> Came whiffling through the tulgey wood,
> And burbled as it came!
>
> One, two! One, two! And through and through
> The vorpal blade went snicker-snack!
> He left it dead, and with its head
> He went galumphing back.
>
> "And, has thou slain the Jabberwock?
> Come to my arms, my beamish boy!
> O frabjous day! Callooh! Callay!"
> He chortled in his joy.
>
> `Twas brillig, and the slithy toves
> Did gyre and gimble in the wabe:
> All mimsy were the borogoves,
> And the mome raths outgrabe.

The exercise was first to memorize this poem entirely and second to recite this memorized poem in character. For added kicks, each person's 'performance' would be videoed for posterity. The stated reason for the recording was to reference back the initial 'performance' to track growth. We were given one week to prepare ourselves before the 'performances' began. For most of the class, this was the 'worst of all worlds'.

The poem was nonsense, had to be memorized and then recited back while dressed in character! The saving grace was that there was complete interpretative and character freedom. Was this a poem about some epic battle with a mythical beast? Was it a different type of battle with a different type of enemy? What and how could I best interpret this nonsense and then find a way to memorize it?

I don't sing (or at least sing well) and have trouble carrying a tune, but to me this seemed to be the rhythmic pattern of a song. My strategy was to find a way to put this poem to the same tune as a familiar song. It would then be much easier to memorize and recite than simple rote memorization. In other words, I would interpret someone else's work creatively with the pattern of someone else's song. Placing together two distinct and disparate patterns would create a new and original entity. But I still had to choose a song and make it work.

The obvious choice was *Puff the Magic Dragon* (Peter, Paul and Mary, 1963). After all, it seemed to me that the mythical beast was dragon-esque. Unfortunately, the rhythm and timing of this classic wouldn't work here. Try as I might, I couldn't make it flow. It was just as well, since I couldn't imagine trying to find a suit of armor or a dragon costume and then actually wearing it. So I was back to square one and this time with just a few remaining days to put it all together.

At around the same time, I was digging through a closet at home, when I chanced upon a ten-gallon cowboy hat. I don't remember where it came from or how it got there, but suddenly a 'crazy' idea popped in my head. What if I used the theme music from the Lone Ranger (the *William Tell Overture*, Rossini, 1829)? It had varying tunes and speeds that flowed well together. It also would provide me my interpretation and character. I would be the Lone Ranger, complete with hat, mask and even cap guns for additional effect. The beast would be some villain that could be summarily dispatched by our hero. I asked myself, "Why the hell not?"

I asked myself, "what is the worst that could happen?" At that time, other than brief introductions, I knew no one else in the class. If I embarrassed myself with a poor performance, at least I wouldn't have to hear about it forever. Besides, I could always burn the tape after the class was over. (Ironically, now that I would like to view it again, I can't seem to locate the tape, despite my best detective efforts.)

I practiced (and practiced and practiced some more) until I felt I could at least recite the whole poem from memory. I even had a great introduction before launching, "Lewis Carroll and Rossini lived at the same time. I don't know if they ever met or collaborated together, but if they did, I imagine it would go something like this. . ." And then I launched into the song. The class and instructor loved it, I got positive laughter (at heart, I'm still a class clown) and received an 'A' for the work. I never had so much fun being out of my comfort zone and I believe the experience helped launch my public speaking efforts.

Creativity and innovation thrive on new uses for established things (adaptive change) and creating something completely new (radical change). Either way, the status quo is disrupted and will typically lead to even more new ideas and innovations. The emphasis should always be on 'new'. It could be completely new to the world or just new to you. It could be an actual product or process, but either way it all starts with some sort of new perspective.

Key takeaways:
1) *Patterned thought is, and has been, a part of our everyday thought processes since we were children.*
2) *Creative thought requires departing from our set and known patterns.*
3) *Breaking out of patterned thought doesn't necessarily mean that we can't use patterns in different and, possibly, unintended ways.*
4) *When we think of originality, it doesn't have to be a brand new invention (aka reinventing the wheel) rather it could simply be a new-to-us use for an established (or patterned) product or process.*

PRINCIPLE 5
CREATE NEW
PERSPECTIVES

In the spirit of the *Reader's Digest* series, *See the world in a different light,* I present the following: What and/or where is this?

While this picture represents an actual entity and is located in a specific place, it really could be anything and anywhere we want it to be. It doesn't really matter what it actually is or even where it actually is, just what and where we perceive and imagine it to be. I won't spoil the surprise (just yet), suffice to say this presents a new perspective on an established thing.

The great thing about our brains is that they are already primed to be creative and to think creatively. We can be going about our everyday lives and suddenly, something will pop up, trigger the senses and get us thinking. We just have to allow ourselves this departure from our routine and patterned thought.

We all started off with this ability as children. Consider a baby or toddler who looks with wonder at every new sight. It is a brand new world unsullied by assumption or previously conceived perception. It truly is whatever and however he or she sees it. As the child grows and gains cognitive ability, we guide him or her as to what he or she is seeing. Gradually, the world takes on some sort of order. But there still lies the explorative side. Children are naturally curious and seek out new things and information. Sometimes, the curiosity leads to trouble, but it is all part of the learning process.

We previously referenced a few of my daughter's toys and how they influence both cognitive thoughts and patterns. My daughter, like most young children, loves banging things together to make different noises. One of her toys is a plastic drum sitting on a slightly raised plastic platform.

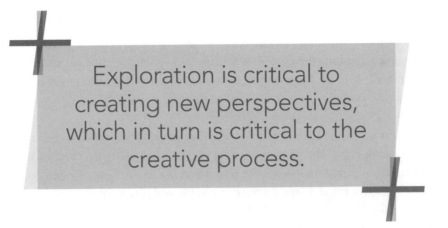

Exploration is critical to creating new perspectives, which in turn is critical to the creative process.

While she enjoys picking up the drum stick and banging it on the drum and other nearby objects, she has also discovered that if she flips the drum upside down, it makes a very different sound. Furthermore, she has discovered, much to her enjoyment, that if she stands on the upside down drum and then stomps on it with her feet, that it makes yet another sound. Would we normally think to play a drum using either of these non-conventional methods?

As we progress into adulthood, we are encouraged to be efficient and responsible. While this is expected and seemingly proper, we somehow lose our 'explorer's hats' and become engrossed with routine. And the longer we're engaged in routine, the more dulled our senses become. We might pass something truly amazing and not even notice. The only exception to this might be those people who pursue certain hobbies (such as hiking, rafting, snowmobiling). For these people, the adventure is directly linked to the exploration.

While I am not encouraging (or discouraging) anyone to take on these adventurous activities, I am encouraging exploration. Exploration is critical to creating new perspectives, which in turn is critical to the creative process.

A new perspective can be gained by using our five senses differently towards a particular object, process and/or challenge. A new perspective can also be gained by using a different sense than the conventional when considering new ideas and topics.

Two of our previous exercises had enhancement potential through use of new perspectives. For instance, in our brick exercise, we perceive the brick by looking at it (sight) and using our experience and knowledge to form opinions, assumptions and ideas. Where else might we see bricks of any sort? What do those look like? What should they look like? Even more importantly, what could they look like?

Moving on to our hearing sense, what could be gained by hearing how the brick sounds? If we dropped the brick on different objects and noted the differing sounds, what might pop in our heads? If we banged the brick against different objects, might we notice something else? Might different bricks of different sizes and shapes make different sounds?

How many of us thought to touch the brick? Is there anything that could be gained by noting what type of texture it has, or could have? Does the texture itself conjure up memories or usage ideas? What if we let our minds wander to other types of bricks or stones or even bricks made of foam and plastic? Could that possibly inspire that next great idea?

What about smelling the brick? There is a distinct smell associated with masonry. If we consider bricks made of foam and or plastics, there certainly is a distinct and recognizable smell. Are those smells evocative of something else? And could that something else lead us on the path to idea discovery?

Of course, the last sense (taste) might be difficult with a conventional, or even a foam or plastic brick (unless you favor chipped teeth and relish the gag reflex). But even here, consider a brick of cheese or chocolate. These tastes are distinctive and should easily provoke thoughts of times, places and people. Is there an innovative notion nestled within these thoughts?

There are two other senses, albeit not necessarily conventional ones: humor and imagination.

There is no limit to what can be unleashed and accelerated when we are laughing and simply enjoying life. In what humorous and crazy ways could we use this brick? Just remember that 'crazy' is subjective and even if an idea truly is 'out there', there is likely something that can be taken away and used practically. After all, humor always has some truth element enclosed, which is why we can relate to it.

Imagination can be used for humor and for more serious ventures too. Leaving aside the humor element, and after we have explored what the conventional senses might tell us, what might we then dream about? Do we have any notions of what this brick could do or be?

The purpose of using all, or a combination of, our senses is twofold. One, we need to open ourselves up to new perspectives. These can only be gained through using our senses. The second reason involves elimination of bias (or assumptions).

We are all biased in one form or another as to how the world, its people and its components operate and should operate. When it comes to ethnicity or religion, we refer to this as ethnocentricity. This complex sociological concept is really a simple way of saying that we believe the world revolves around our own ethnic or religious groups. This concept has profound influence on our perceptions and assumptions. While I don't intend to delve further into this type of bias, it's important to note its influence and to recognize that bias is also significant in ideas, processes, perceptions and assumptions.

In the scientific community, there is a general rule (specifically in regard to statistical analysis): Random is magic. Random selection processes must be used otherwise normal everyday bias has the possibility of corrupting the study. Randomness should also be applied as a rule to any statistical study, especially surveys. We all see the results of endless surveys, especially during election season (and when isn't it election season?).

"2,000 random voters were surveyed with an error margin of +/- 3%"; "A poll of 400 likely voters found that..." and of course, (leaving politics momentarily) who can forget, "four out of five dentists/doctors/vets recommend..."?

Let's say that the pool of people surveyed were selected in a statistically random fashion. And let's also assume (which we must do absent any other information) that the number of people surveyed is statistically significant as compared to the total population affected. We must then ask if the question asked is also free of bias?

How the question is phrased and asked is of critical importance to the result. I can have my survey show any preconceived result simply by tinkering with the words of the question, the medium via which it is asked and, of course, the tone of voice, inflection, volume and emphasis of the questioner. This concept is also critically important to our personal bias and how we perceive the world.

We are all biased in one form or another as to how the world, its people and its components operate and should operate.

Let's take another look at the brick to better illustrate bias in action.

We see the brick and immediately think "building material". We don't naturally think weapon or projectile, as our bias isn't in that direction. Conversely, if we saw a gun we would immediately think "weapon" due to our bias. We wouldn't naturally think of the gun as a planter or flag holder for the same reason; our bias isn't in that direction.

We see the brick and immediately think "rust red" color. We don't naturally think "green" or "purple" or even "blue". We see the brick and instantly think "hefty" and "weighty". We don't naturally think "hollow" or "lightweight material". We certainly don't naturally think bricks of cheese or chocolate. All of this is due to our bias; in this case, towards the conventional uses, colors and dimensions.

When an organization retains me to examine processes, I don't have a bias. I am unclouded and unfettered by any of the politics, people or other considerations. For the sake of the examination, I consider myself dumb and uneducated. Certainly, the 5-Why process helps here, but even without that process, I require explanations for each step. If it can't be explained to me relatively quickly and in normal everyday words, there are problems lurking.

We are frequently unaware of the impact our bias has in our normal thinking. The problem is amplified by the difficulty we have in accurate self-assessment. We're too close to the problem and we have too much invested in hearing whatever we want to hear, seeing what we want to see and believing what we want to believe. This is especially prevalent in creative pursuits.

Returning to our ice cream stick exercise, bias again played a major role in how groups reacted to this challenge. The notches on the stick indicated that they must be used in the conventional way (one stick fits into another). Our bias told us, "the notches are there for a reason". Our bias told us, "no, we cannot use anything else to help us assemble this structure". Our bias also told us, "no, we cannot break the sticks to help us; they must remain whole".

What happens is that some groups are victimized by their own internal biases, despite the fact that no direction has been given disallowing alternate means. When the exercise is over, these same groups are offended by those that ignored their bias and said, "Why the hell not?" They are offended by the groups that used tape or glue, the groups that placed sticks on top of tall objects, the groups

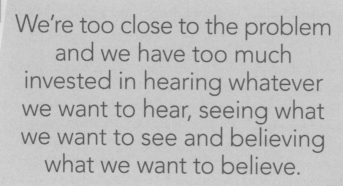

> We're too close to the problem and we have too much invested in hearing whatever we want to hear, seeing what we want to see and believing what we want to believe.

that broke and bent their sticks to help support their structures and finally, the groups that assembled their structure flat on the table. Their thought process is, "Hey, they cheated!"

In a way, they are right. However, these groups didn't cheat the system; they cheated their own bias inclination. Gaining new perspectives requires continuous cheating and ignoring of our own bias inclinations. Without it, our bias takes over and we're left with nothing but conventional thoughts, wondering why creativity is so elusive.

While there are many methods of gaining new perspectives, I will typically employ one that also generates laughter. I strongly believe that if we are smiling and laughing and, even when contemplating a serious issue, we allow ourselves greater freedom of thought.

At some point, we've probably all played a game of Mad Libs (Price Stern Sloan – Penguin) and enjoyed the unexpected resulting hilarity. For those uninitiated, Mad Libs is a series of word games, where the participants provide nouns, verbs, adjectives, adverbs, and so on, in sequential order. Each word is then plugged into a story template. For instance, the template might read, "After I left the (noun), I (verb/past tense) with the (noun). Inevitably, the resulting story becomes ridiculously funny. This is a popular party/group game and never fails to generate intense laughter.

But can it be used in a keynote speech to a large group of people not expecting to play a game? Conventional wisdom (also known as bias) would indicate not, but my response is... "Why the hell not?" And together, the audience and I continue...

The great thing about playing this game during a keynote is that many people realize what is going on, realize they are being had and yet willingly go along for the ride. I have yet to receive an adverse response while doing this in a speech or workshop, or from identified or anonymous feedback afterwards.

While we are getting everybody laughing and having a good time, it serves a distinct creative purpose as well; it creates new perspectives. When we assemble sentences in non-conventional ways using words that initially don't seem to make much sense, we cannot help but stimulate the idea generator in our brains. The ideas might not have much practicality, but they serve as an impetus to other ideas that could be used. It's all about creating new perspectives and I have no boundaries or rules in the pursuit of sharing this with everyone I encounter.

Other exercises to stimulate creation of new perspectives include reverse thinking and random word exercises. Reverse thinking is a proven method for moving the discussion beyond conventional thinking. Let's consider a sample problem; creating an effective sales-generating website.

> While we are getting everybody laughing and having a good time, it serves a distinct creative purpose as well; it creates new perspectives.

Certainly, there are enough available resources touting tried-and-tested methods, verbiage and phraseology. But let's say that we've tried any number of these methods and in different combinations, all with limited effectiveness. We want more from our website, but how do we get it?

What if we started thinking of all the ways we could make the website a complete sales disaster? What if we started thinking and recording all the ways we could alienate (and when I say alienate, I don't mean merely annoy or inconvenience) our existing customers and scare off any new ones? What if we started thinking of all the ways our website could elicit negative publicity and lots of it?

When we are done with thinking and recording/writing down all the ways to make the website a disaster, we can now reverse those thoughts to discover positive ways of improving the site. For instance, let's say, during the exercise, we included the statement, "we'll take all your money and run away". We can now include language that attests to our strong ethics and reliability. If during the exercise, we said, "our products and services don't work and are guaranteed to create many sleepless nights and executive-induced wedgies", we can now include testimonials from clients who love the product and can attest to its true worth. Perhaps we can even move away from just 'tooting our own horn', instead, opting to let our actions (and what others have to say about them) do the heavy-lifting (reverse of providing negative and inflammatory quotes about our product).

Random words work in a similar fashion. By placing together words that are randomly generated (special emphasis on random), we create new ways of looking at our problems and issues. There is no limit to the type or severity of the problem that can be addressed using a random words exercise. The key is that, by thinking on a different plane, we are able to go somewhere we might not otherwise have gone (all puns intended). And by going somewhere new, we are able to evoke new and different perspectives leading to new ideas to help solve the problem.

Speaking about fresh perspectives, do you remember the picture I presented earlier and the question asked? Here it is again with the question being what and/or where is this?

First hint: It is somewhere in the Greater Midwest US (includes Minnesota, Iowa, Missouri, Illinois, Wisconsin, Michigan, Indiana and Ohio).

Second hint: It is considered a structure.

Key Takeaways:
1) Opening ourselves up to new perspectives can only be gained through usage of our senses.
2) Gaining new perspectives requires continuous cheating and ignoring our own bias inclinations.
3) By using laughter and/or random word exercises, we are able to gain new perspectives on even intractable issues.

PRINCIPLE 6
MINIMIZE NEGATIVE THINKING

On the subject of bias inclination, there is another type of bias that frequently interferes with our ability to generate new ideas creatively. But first, a quick question? Are you an optimist, pessimist or something in between? If you said realist, that's not sufficiently definite. You can be a realistic optimist, a realistic pessimist or a realistic blend.

The next time you're in a meeting and new ideas are being offered, sit back and observe the proceedings. If you note that, when an idea is offered, it is quickly judged, probably in a negative fashion, then you have observed our overwhelming bias to treat an unknown negatively. It doesn't matter how we view ourselves, we tend to resort to negative thinking when something new is offered up.

Sometimes we mask the negativity by engaging in semantics. We say that we are being realists and simply offering constructive criticism. We say that we must view these ideas critically or how will we know if they're truly sustainable? Unfortunately, what we are really doing is violating our first rule of creative process: to separate idea generation from evaluation. But even more importantly, we are harvesting negativity, and negativity is very fertile ground.

Like a field filled with weeds and invasive plants where there is no room for productive plants, with negativity there is no room for ideas. Productive and desired ideas are choked by the insatiable appetite of ravenously negative reactions.

In every workshop I give, I poll participants on a common business problem/ issue. I then solicit ideas from the same participants with the caveat that anyone can interject their opinion, positive or negative, at any time after hearing the idea. Thankfully, most audiences are relatively polite in that they won't suddenly interject, instead opting to raise their hands and waiting to be heard. However, I have noticed eyes rolling at certain ideas, occasional whispering between people and the politely worded criticism when someone is called on to speak out. I have rarely heard a positive, encouraging or reinforcing interjection.

Is it that we don't want to be supportive and/or reassuring? Or are we really exposing our fear of the unknown? Or is it that our bias inclination is returning for another helping?

Actually, all three are simultaneously in play.

There are two reasons why we might not want to show support or reassurance publicly. The first is that we don't want to appear weak. Somehow, in the business world, making reinforcing, supportive comments is considered weak (except if it is the boss's or senior executive's idea) while negative comments are considered strong. Second, we don't want to show support for something that isn't a sure thing. In other words, we are not yet willing to assume risk by supporting this currently untested, unsanctioned and/or unvetted idea.

> If it's too difficult to aggregate all the ideas before jumping into evaluation and selection, couldn't we inquire how a solution might work, even if it, at face-value, seems truly impractical?

We are also definitely afraid of the unknown. This fear can be debilitating and prevent any meaningful progress or idea generation. Our defense mechanism is to attack the instigator of the unknown in the hope that the status quo will remain. We'll roll our eyes and make critical comments. We'll excuse these actions by stating that we're just looking out for the company.

In reality, we are just looking out for ourselves and these actions are self-defense manifestations. While we are doing this, our brain is on high alert and cannot possibly be in any sort of idea generation mode. We have effectively shut off the new idea spigot.

Finally, we are biased in favor of our perception of the problem and the possible solution. We frequently parrot "consider things with an open mind". Even if we surmise that we could be open to ideas that might directly conflict with our established thinking and conclusions, could we also then be supportive of these? Furthermore, most of us perceive this prerogative to be about considering multiple ideas simultaneously in the effort to choose the optimal idea.

Unfortunately, we don't multitask very well (if at all). So instead, we listen to one idea, immediately evaluate it under our bias microscope, and either reject it for 'good reason' or accept it (probably corresponding to our own held opinions and biases). We will sometimes do this before the idea has even been fully communicated. We hear part of the idea, immediately fill in the blanks, evaluate and, in all probability, discard it.

All of this serves to reinforce our negativity bias, and when we are negative, there is no room for the competing thoughts of idea generation.

The solution is simple, yet very difficult to achieve. Instead of automatically evaluating ideas under the prism of "why it won't work", let's switch the prism to "how can we make it work?"

For instance, if we're trying to solve chronic absenteeism in a particular department, shouldn't every idea be given every opportunity to succeed? If it's too difficult to aggregate all the ideas before jumping into evaluation and selection, couldn't we inquire how a solution might work, even if it, at face-value, seems truly impractical?

Let's say the first idea (using our sense of humor) is to throw anyone with an un-excused absence into the dunk tank at the next company picnic. Of course, we could immediately offer up myriad reasons, most legitimate, for why it wouldn't work. But let's say we tried a different tactic. Let's say that we made a sincere effort to making the idea work. Maybe a system of credits and exchanges could be established, so that people who would actually like to be in the dunk tank could switch with those who should have been there. Maybe a system could be fashioned whereby, rather than punishing the offender, additional responsibilities were given to them. The goal would be to reinforce the realization that the offending employee is needed. And so on. By employing a "how could this work" perspective, we are likely to gain new insights into both the issue at hand and to resolving it.

Negativity also manifests itself in everyday communication. When asked, "how are you doing", how often is the response, "not too bad", "can't complain", or "could be worse"? If things are truly going well and we are having a good day, we should answer, "I'm doing well" or "things are going well". Another version of this response is the sarcastic "living the dream". Considering most people don't dream about their work, the unspoken message conveyed is one of routine, drudgery or worse, displeasure.

This isn't just a matter of semantics or word preferences. We are subconsciously projecting how we are truly feeling when we use negative language. "Not too bad" really means that things aren't going quite as well as we might have hoped. "Can't complain" really means that I could complain but I'm choosing not to (at this point in time). Even if said in a jocular manner, we are still projecting subconscious negativity. When we are feeling negative, it is extremely difficult, if not impossible, to think creatively. Our minds simply don't have enough band-width to deal with the negativity and simultaneously be in the positive state that nourishes creative thought.

Unfortunately, there are other common ways in which organizations create negativity or negative engagement. I particularly refer to communications. Aside from the perpetual penchant for under-communication or lack of timely, relevant and honest communication, there are problems with what is actually being communicated.

For example, consider this genuine memo (originating company omitted to protect the guilty):

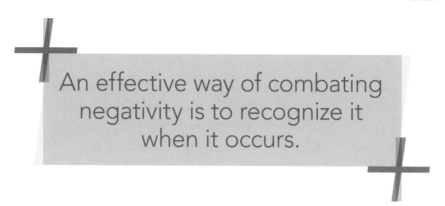

An effective way of combating negativity is to recognize it when it occurs.

"We can undertake with key stakeholders to get some traction with an innovative paradigm shift to contextual mindfulness going forward. At the end of the day, it should be noted that if we can get some alignment, we will have a basis for go-forward renewal within the dynamic thinkspace 2.0. With that framework as the key core strategy painting the new direction, perhaps we could have the discussions at a roundtable, an armchair, or if my time horizon allows, a bilat. That speaks to our ability to demonstrate within a culture of engagement that we have clearly addressed our transformation agenda and met with significant fundamental progress."

Hopefully, this is not a memo that anyone in your company or team would ever send out. If you were the recipient of this corporate double-speak memo, how likely would it inspire immediate (if any) action (other than trying to decipher it)? How likely would it be that this memo might improve your mood or morale?

Communication that obfuscates and confuses is rarely inspirational or motivational (at least not for positive action). In fact, this type of communication is likely to create negative feelings towards the sender. Now, how likely is it that you would be in a frame of mind to be creative, to innovate or problem solve?

We can take this memo and shorten it to three words without losing any of its critical meaning. Those three words, in the spirit of the late comedian and talk-show host, Joan Rivers, would be "Can we talk"?

If the sender had sent those words instead of the confusing memo, it is much more likely that the receiver would respond quickly and in a positive fashion. After all, most of us would be happy to honor this clear and simple request. We would be much more willing to engage, without a negative mindset. And we avoid this negative mindset through frequent, timely, relevant, honest, and most importantly, clear communication (more on this later).

An effective way of combating negativity is to recognize it when it occurs. After recognizing the negative word or thought, we can label it as negative. Then, by invoking a positive method, using positive words, we can eliminate the negative. Try this at home (or at work): Whenever the opportunity for "can't" and "won't" arises, try substituting "can" and "will". Even if added parameters and conditions are necessary, the tone and attitudes are now positive.

Of course, "can we talk?" is very different from "we need to talk".

The former is a simple, respectful request. Everyone is an equal in this conversation and the question is a direct invitation for ideas and thoughts, most likely to solve a problem. The ensuing conversation is thus primed for the coming up with and offering of new ideas.

By contrast, the latter automatically puts the receiver on the defensive while simultaneously reinforcing the nature of being subordinate to the sender. Usually, when someone states, "we need to talk", something is amiss and the blame game quickly ensues. And once the blame game is afoot, our natural reaction is to defend ourselves and our actions. In other words, we are now in a defensive mode (internal claxons blaring, all hands on deck). When we are on the defensive, we are on high alert and tend to be extremely cautious and risk-adverse. This is not the ideal environment for creative thought.

Key takeaways:
1) *All ideas are good ideas as they are the springboards and triggers for further thought, discussion and consideration.*
2) *By thinking positively, our thoughts and idea generating capabilities are limitless and infinite.*
3) *When we focus on how it's possible to achieve ideas, rather than why they will not or cannot work, the possibilities are infinite. The sky is not the limit; it's just the beginning.*

PRINCIPLE 7
TAKE (PRUDENT) RISKS

Unfortunately, limitless and infinite also implies an unknown commodity, which subsequently creates a possible fear component. We are afraid of the unknown. We don't know what it portends, what it means or how it might impact us. Essentially, we are afraid to delve into the unknown, even when it pertains to idea generation. It presents a risk, even if we can't quantify or understand its nature. We must be able to acknowledge and manage this risk if we wish to experience breakthroughs.

If we stopped to consider our everyday activities, we would realize that there are both overt and subtle risks with most of our activities. We could, if we really wanted to, quantify the risks associated with each of these activities (for example, making coffee poses the risk of an electric malfunction and a risk presented by the hot water itself; taking a shower poses a risk of slipping on the wet surface and being scalded by hot water; driving to work poses considerable risks relating to all types of accidents, and so on).

We are confronting risks every day, yet most of us somehow manage to emerge unscathed. We may even specifically acknowledge some of these risks without fleeing from the risky activity. Why, then, are we able to confront these risks, which pose potential considerable harm to life and limb, but unable to confront other, less insidious risks?

The answer probably lies in that trusty self-defense mechanism known as denial. While we acknowledge there is an overall risk, we think it couldn't happen to us. We will take all the necessary precautions with the nastier risks and subjugate the others to remote possibilities unlikely to ever happen. We are big proponents of probability over possibility. Could it possibly happen? Yes. Is it likely to happen? No. We then continue on with our daily routines.

In actuality, this mentality is quite productive when it comes to routines. After all, if we worried about every potential risk and took every possible precaution to avoid it, we wouldn't get anywhere or accomplish anything. We similarly subconsciously (sometimes consciously) divide these risks into prudent and non-prudent (or excessive risks). Taking a shower while not making any sudden moves on a slippery floor would be considered a prudent risk, while taking a shower standing on your head or while learning the latest dance club moves would probably be considered a non-prudent risk. Driving to work in a relatively non-distracted fashion and within the speed limit would be considered a prudent risk, while driving to work at high speed, while texting, emailing or shaving would be considered a non-prudent risk.

We must continuously take prudent risks or we would never go anywhere or do anything. We certainly wouldn't innovate, create or change anything. Advances originally from somebody somewhere taking a chance on an idea; someone daring to challenge assumptive thought; someone willing to confront change's risks prudently and still charge forward.

In a recent conversation with Walter E Pasko, Vice President - Procurement for Valmont Industries (one of the world's leading providers of engineered products and services for infrastructure and irrigation equipment for agriculture), the dangers of improper risk assessments were made clear. He relayed his experience as an IT project manager for McDonalds, working on a vendor management project. Somewhere in the process, a concern was raised about the possibility of duplicate vendor entries but with slightly different spellings; a common occurrence with multiple users entering data. The concern was summarily dismissed as an impossibility; something that couldn't happen. Naturally, the project became bogged down when there was found a proliferation of duplicate vendor entries with slightly different spellings.

Walter further talked about a historical occurrence of proper risk assessment and planning; namely General Patton's planning ahead of the Battle of the Bulge in

We must continuously take prudent risks or we would never go anywhere or do anything. We certainly wouldn't innovate, create or change anything.

World War II. While it seemed unlikely that the German Panzer tank divisions could mobilize and counter-attack through the Ardennes, he planned for its occurrence. When it did happen, he was able to react quickly and decisively to prevent lasting damage.

"Always cover your down-side" is the strategy Walter conveys, specifically in terms of evaluating as many potential risks, or risk families, as possible. One can never have blinders on, regarding potential setbacks and since there will always be setbacks, planning, and never assuming, becomes urgent and critical. Furthermore, with any initiative planning, there must be an immediate alternative on which to fall back, in case the original plan doesn't work. This alternate planning must include and document processes, procedures and suppliers (both internal and external) so that an initiative failure can be seamlessly transitioned with a minimal amount of chaotic damage.

The key to breaking through the innovation risk barrier can be as simple as a risk-reward comparison. What is the worst thing that could happen from daring to think of new ideas? What is the worst thing that could happen if all of the ideas were deemed to be impractical, unrealistic and/or unworkable? What is the worst thing that could happen by not immediately judging or filtering any of the ideas before recording them?

But before we can really answer these questions, we have to ask ourselves another one: What does prudent really mean and does it mean the same thing for different people?

There is no question that when it pertains to risk and risk tolerance/aversion, there are significant differences between people and organizations. As a professional general aviation pilot, I can personally attest to these differences in action.

Commonly accepted statistics show that one is more likely to be injured or killed driving to the airport than when travelling on a commercial flight. The key words here are commercial flight. The airlines have rigorous flight crew training and fully tested, recorded and implemented crew resource management systems that drive safe processes throughout. It is these systems and processes that drive down the potential risks. While there will always be some risk, this risk is quite manageable and one that most people are willing to assume.

> There is no question that when it pertains to risk and risk tolerance/aversion, there are significant differences between people and organizations.

But when it comes to general aviation (non-commercial), the numbers are very different. The risks inherent in a general aviation flight are significantly higher than the risks inherent in driving to the airport. The differences are mostly attributable to differences in training and in quality/maintenance of the aircraft itself. To be clear, general aviation is quite safe and becoming even safer. It is just not as safe as commercial aviation.

There are many people who would not wish to assume this additional risk. Does this avoidance mean that taking a general aviation flight is not a prudent risk? Of course, the answer depends on who you ask. For my passengers and me, it is a prudent risk, manageable by considerable pre-flight inspections, meticulous weather briefings and frequent/recurrent training. For others, the risk is too high and would thus be considered a non-prudent risk.

So if prudence of risk is subjective, how can we best define and quantify it?

We can simply define risk as the probability that a hazard will occur. A hazard is an event or circumstance that potentially imperils the success of the goal. For instance, if our goal is to drive 500 miles from Chicago, IL to Memphis, TN and arrive as quickly as possible, a hazard could be inclement road conditions that either slow us down or force us to halt the journey temporarily. The risk (or probability of not reaching the goal) would naturally be higher in winter and lower in summer.

Another hazard could be active state trooper patrols along the route, forcing a stricter compliance with official speed limits. The risk here is harder to quantify and relates to the position and number of officers along the route and varying enforcement patterns at different periods. Certainly, there will be portions of the trip where there will be little to no coverage, but finding out where these are might be difficult. Perhaps near the end of the month (ticket quotas – or as one of my defense attorney friends says – minimums), during daylight hours (when there is more traffic on the road, more troopers on shift), we could view the risk as higher than it would be at the beginning of the month during nighttime hours. Thus, in theory, higher probability of a hazard occurrence means greater risk and vice versa.

However, not all hazards and risks are equal and the above scenario calculates risk using a mix of subjective and objective information. We must be able to sort through potential hazards and risks by impact on the initiative. A common method to quantify risk objectively is through utilization of a risk matrix.

Below is a simple version of a risk matrix.

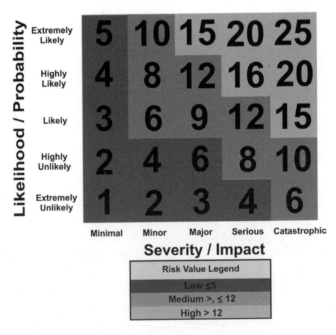

Let's now return to our scenario: A 500-mile road trip from Chicago to Memphis with the goal to arrive as quickly as possible. We have identified two potential hazards: inclement weather and active state trooper patrols. While there are other potential hazards (mechanical trouble, motion sickness), for simplicity, we'll just use the first stated hazard, inclement weather.

The hazard of inclement weather along the route can potentially slow us down or even temporarily stop the journey. What is the likelihood of this happening? Assume that the weather forecast is mixed. There are surrounding areas of clear, light precipitation and heavy precipitation. The next question is what type of precipitation? Is it snow, freezing rain, sleet, or just rain? Undoubtedly, the time of year is a critical factor. Based on the forecast and time of year (early spring), we say that it is somewhat likely that we'll encounter typical inclement weather for the season (rain, fog, and so on).

Now, we need to quantify the impact of this inclement weather should we be delayed or even stopped. The real question is how arriving later than planned would impact upon us. We need to identify the reason(s) for our trip. Is it for a wedding or an important meeting? Is it for a sporting event? Is it to meet family or friends for a visit or vacation? The impact of being late will vary. If it's absolutely critical that we arrive on schedule (for example, for an important meeting), the impact of not arriving on time will be significantly higher. If it is our preference that we arrive on time (for a sporting event, perhaps), but it will only be annoying if we don't arrive on time, then the impact will be more moderate. Finally, the resulting impact will be much lower if our potential late arrival creates little-to-no adversity (family visit/vacation).

The following rundown better illustrates proper use of the matrix, assuming we have concluded that it is very likely we will encounter inclement weather:

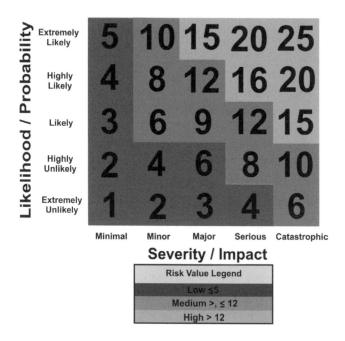

95

Some quick matrix notes: The vertical axis labeled 'likelihood' can also be understood as 'probability'. In other words, what is the probability that a hazard will be encountered. For example, if we are referring to inclement weather for the trip and we determine that is very likely, we will find very likely on the vertical axis and highlight that horizontal line across the matrix.

We will then determine the severity/impact of us being late for the meeting/event (the reason for our trip). If the impact is minimal (getting together with family or friends), we will locate 'minimal' on the severity/impact (horizontal) axis and highlight that vertical line across the matrix. Where the two highlighted lines meet, we have a numeric value. The higher the value (number) the greater the assumed risk for the trip. By using the risk value legend directly below the severity/impact axis, we can then estimate our overall risk for the trip.

On the vertical axis (likelihood), we identify 'Highly likely' and then look for the corresponding category on the horizontal axis (severity/impact).

Family visit/vacation will have a 'minimal' impact if we arrive later than expected due to the inclement weather. This gives us a risk value of four. If we then refer to the risk value legend, we will determine that the risk value of four presents a low risk factor.

Wedding/sporting event will have a 'minor' impact if we arrive later than expected due to the inclement weather. This gives us a risk value of eight or a medium risk factor.

Finally, 'important meeting' will have either a 'serious' or 'catastrophic' impact if we arrive later than expected (or not at all) due to the inclement weather. This gives us a risk value of either 16 or 20, which makes this a high risk factor.

While this is a more formal method of ascertaining risk, we go through these calculations informally in our everyday lives. Whenever we are trying to decide what to do or not do, we figure out what risk is present, whether we are comfortable with that risk, what we might do to mitigate that risk and finally, a go/no-go decision. After all, we don't really need the risk matrix to decide when and where to cross the street.

The downside to the everyday informal method is that it can be quite prone to subjectivity and bias. Some of us have different thresholds of risk obtained through experience and/or prevailing opinion. And while experience is an excellent teacher, prevailing opinion may or may not be the appropriate yardstick to measure risk.

So now let's once again use the matrix to quantify idea generation risk:

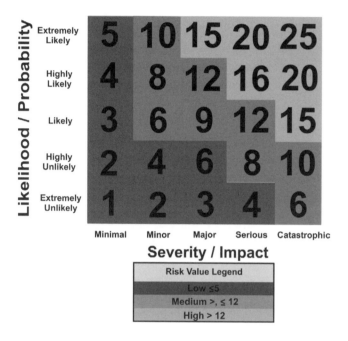

An honest examination will unearth the following likely risks: A temporary loss of face (if others are too quick to judge the idea) or perhaps missing that next great idea (if we, ourselves, are too quick to judge and do not share our ideas).

A temporary loss of face is likely to have a minimal or minor severity/impact on idea generation due to its temporary nature. Its probability will also be low, since everyone involved is presumably in the same idea-generation process. Thus, everyone involved has the 'keeping each other honest' mentality. The objective matrix will allow us to conclude that this is a low risk factor and thus would be a prudent risk.

For the contrarians, let's assume that this loss of face is likely. If we say that the impact is minimal, the risk is still low (risk factor three) and even if the impact is minor (risk factor six), the risk barely crosses the line to medium. Thus, the idea-generation process is a risk worth taking, if for no other reason than the alternative poses risks not worth taking.

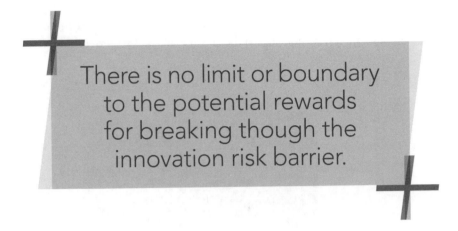

There is no limit or boundary to the potential rewards for breaking though the innovation risk barrier.

Now let's examine the risk involved with the alternative to the idea generation process: missing that next great idea. If we speculatively calculate that the impact would be major and that the corresponding hazard (of looking foolish) is very unlikely, (risk factor value of three) the risk would be considered prudent. If we say that the hazard (of looking foolish) is likely, then we are solidly in the moderate risk (risk factor value of nine). However, not suggesting the next great idea with a low risk factor value of three is really a risk of inaction, which means that it is the same risk as not generating ideas and/or following the creative process. It is no worse than not changing anything.

By using the risk matrix with these examples, we can see that missing that next great idea will not impact anything since without it, there will be no change. Therefore, we can reasonably conclude that generating ideas by allowing the creative process to work is a low-to-moderate risk. I believe that this would constitute a prudent risk and would certainly be worth undertaking.

Now that we've ascertained that it's a low-to-moderate risk, let's look at the potential rewards of being able to break through the innovation risk barrier. We will do this in an effort to quantify a positive risk-reward ratio (with the potential reward greatly outweighing the potential risk).

We might gain a reputation as someone who can innovate and be creative, even with seemingly mundane topics and concepts. We might think of that next great product or process idea that will help propel the company forward, improve operational efficiencies and positively impact the bottom line overall. We might inspire someone else on the team to come up with that next great idea. We might inspire the group, or even the entire company, to think of that next great idea. There is no limit or boundary to the potential rewards for breaking though the innovation risk barrier.

If we complete our risk-reward comparison, it's clear that the rewards infinitely outweigh the risks for generating new ideas without fear of adversity. In the idea-generating phase there should be no artificial barriers or boundaries. Any and all ideas thought of and verbalized should be recorded without bias or prejudging. At this stage, all idea-generation risks are prudent, regardless of applicability.

Key Takeaways:

1) Acknowledging that not all risks are created equal is critical to the creative process.

2) Using an objective method (such as the risk matrix), idea generation poses little substantive risk.

3) Using a risk-reward comparison the potential rewards of idea generation greatly outweigh any potential risks.

PRINCIPLE 8
GET LOST!

One of the many delights of parenthood is sharing the joys of discovery with your child. With my three older children, I was less attuned to this discovery phase than I am currently. Looking back, I find it ironic that discovery and explorer dad wasn't recognizing the joy of discovery that was present in their everyday lives. Thankfully, with my almost two-year-old daughter, I am right with her as she discovers the world around her.

To her, the entire world is wide open and just waiting for her to observe and experience. It doesn't matter if it's a run in the back yard, down the street, a trip to a farm or even walking around a room in someone else's house. It is all new and exciting to her and in many ways, I envy her. Of course, when her discovery causes trouble (her 'real' middle name) it is difficult for me to be too upset. After all, this is all part of her discovery and her version of Intelligent Fast Failure. (Quick reminder: Intelligent Fast Failure is taking rapid limited experiments to eliminate quickly what doesn't work and to reinforce what does work. In this regard, failures are an integral part of the ultimate successful process). It takes diligent effort to guide my daughter's discoveries to accentuate the positives and minimize the negatives. After all, the last thing I would want to do is squash her discovering.

But somehow, as we grow older, life's responsibilities and our better understanding of risks and reciprocal actions take us further and further away from those unbridled discovery days. Even though I personally enjoy rafting down a river for the first time, hiking a new path or even piloting my plane to a destination I've never visited, I feel less likely to go boldly in a new direction than in years past. Perhaps this is why I relish landing at new airports for the first time. To me, this is discovery and exploration, albeit in a quasi-controlled environment.

I also recall a particular trip taken with a friend in the days pre-GPS (only 20 years ago) where the only directives were that we would travel on non-interstate roads, heading either north or west. We had maps with us but they were banished to the glove compartment, not to be consulted until we decided to return home. My buddy Jake and I left Chicago on a Monday morning, and three days later, found ourselves in Miles City, Montana.

Along the way, we discovered fantastic little towns with odd claims to fame (one town announced on its welcome sign: 654 people and one old grump); crossed over the majestic Missouri river in South Dakota; had the run of Mount Rushmore practically to ourselves; hiked partially up Devils Tower in Wyoming (a prominent rock formation in the Eastern Rocky Mountains) and visited Home on the Range, North Dakota (named after the folk song). It was one of the best trips I have ever taken, comparing favorably with more exotic destinations. We never consulted any map and just took whatever road we fancied, truly exploring and discovering for the entire trip.

So here's the challenge to recreating this discovery, albeit without the risk of actually getting lost: First, turn off the GPS in your vehicle and don't consult the GPS on your smartphone (you could always turn it back on to navigate home). Then set off on any road in any direction and just keep going. The trip could be an hour, a day or however long you wish to travel. The world outside your familiarity zone beckons. What will you find and/or discover? What new or creative thoughts might be inspired as a result?

Getting lost doesn't have to involve a physical journey. We can get lost in a good book, listening to music, even while eating a delicious meal. All of these serve the purpose of damping the active conscious and with that, accentuating the sudden awareness of everything the subconscious has to offer.

Furthermore, all of these activities, and especially music, are likely to trigger memories and thoughts about people, places and things from the past. Any of us could probably listen to a particular song and immediately be reminded of another time. Perhaps we are reminded of something or someone present when we first heard the song, or perhaps there is a special memory that goes with the song. We are especially attached to songs. Our personal playlists cannot help but conjure up these warm, happy memories. The resulting feelings are likely to inspire our subconscious minds, so that the idea spigot is turned on and running rapidly.

There is more to music than simply getting lost in songs and memories. I started an experiment several years ago regarding personal theme songs. We can all

The world outside your familiarity zone beckons. What will you find and/or discover? What new or creative thoughts might be inspired as a result?

probably hear theme music/songs from certain television shows and instantly recognize the program. Further introduction is unnecessary as we immediately recall everything we used to know about the show, its premise, actors and so on.

Using this premise, I have asked people I know the following question: If a certain music or a particular song could play prior to your entry into a room, and upon hearing the music, everyone in the room would instantly associate it with you, what would that song be? In other words, what is your personal theme song?

This question can provoke considerable thought. First, we need to assess ourselves honestly, consider our personality and that 'special something' that uniquely identifies us. Then we need to reframe that in terms of how other people view us. Finally, we need to marry the two together, and identify a song/music that captures that conjoined view. The answer should be sufficiently obvious both to you and your friends/family/acquaintances so that assent is assured and no further explanation is necessary.

In other words, to answer this question, we need to undertake three distinct discoveries. They are self-discovery, discovery of self as viewed by others, and musical discovery.

For some people, the answer will be quick and obvious. For others, the answer may be quick but not obvious. Remember, if it's not obvious, then the discovery has not unearthed an optimal answer. In some ways, this is comparable to a joke. If it needs to be explained, it's not very funny. The answer should require no further explanation. For others, the answer will be neither quick nor obvious. In fact, I have still not received an answer from some of the people I've previously asked (was it something I said?).

In all fairness, and in an effort to clarify the concept of personal theme songs, I will demonstrate by revealing my personal theme song. But first, let's go through the discovery process.

I have always had an urge to drive much faster than the official speed limits, primarily on interstates, but sometimes even on surface streets. While I long ago tempered the extent of my speeding, I still have difficulty staying at the speed limit, electing to use the unofficial tolerances (up to 10 miles per hour faster than the posted speed limit). In fact, in the past, I have had my driving time between Chicago and other places, such as New York, Baltimore, Louisville and even San

Francisco challenged as not fast enough. Being young and stupid (at the time), I took on the challenges and usually beat the previous times and without a citation. Nowadays, I'm asked why I don't drive as much. The answer isn't that I don't like driving, but that I've found an even faster mode of transportation: flying.

Many of my friends have travelled with me and personally experienced my speeding. I think it is safe to say that speeding is part of who I am and is recognized as such by my family and friends. So what song best personifies this trait? The quick and obvious answer: I Can't Drive 55 by Sammy Hagar (CBS Records, 1983). I have yet to find a friend or family member who doesn't agree that this song is me; in other words, the perfect personal theme song.

Try this one out on yourself and while asking others as well. You will be surprised at what you discover about yourself and what you discover about others.

So if you were to ask me how we could self-inspire ideas, my response would be to get lost!

Now what about our mystery structure located in the Greater Midwest US? Did you guess some sort of sculpture or perhaps part of a building?

What about the Twykenham Avenue Bridge spanning the St Joseph River in South Bend, IN?

Key Takeaways:

1) Allowing ourselves to get lost and discover, whether physically or in thought, allows for creative thought and idea generation.

2) Undertaking the 'personal theme song' challenge evokes considerable thought and self-discovery.

3) Creative inspiration is truly in the senses of the beholder and perceived art is everywhere, if we just allow ourselves to look around and discover.

PRINCIPLE 9
OUT GO
THE LIGHTS

I've always been a big fan of the highly participatory blues song, *Boom Boom – Out Go the Lights* so ably covered by Pat Travers. There is something magical when he prompts the crowd with a "boom-boom" and they respond with an enthusiastic and very loud *'Out Goes the Lights'*. I'm such a big fan that I co-opt this part of the song for many of my talks (of course, giving proper credit to Mr Travers). There is something inspiring and motivating about having an audience full of accomplished and successful people yelling "out go the lights!" If nothing else, I am confidently assured that the audience is fully engaged.

But what does this have to do with creativity?

How about an even better question first?

Why does it seem that our best ideas come in the shower, in the dark, when we're overtired or while we're in some sort of sleep mode?

The technically correct answer is that when we are distracted, tired and/or re-laxed, our prefrontal cortex has diminished power as the base brain network switches on. Meanwhile, our dopamine supplies are greatly increased while the cerebral alpha waves hold sway. Ironically, during this phase, the brain is more active than when we're focused and wide-awake.

Considering that most of us are not brain surgeons well versed in neurotransmitter and cerebral passage knowhow, perhaps I can offer a simpler explanation; it's the lulling of our active conscious state that allows creative thoughts to more easily bypass the 'stupid' filter.

Consider the analogy of driving down a dark road while it's snowing. The only light available is from the car's headlights. The snow falling past the headlights creates the illusion that you are zipping through the snow at a very fast pace. Or if you prefer, consider the televised rendition of warp speed, with the stars and other points of light zipping by at fantastic speeds.

Either example essentially captures what is happening in our brains at any given moment. Millions of diverse and disparate thoughts, notions and ideas are bouncing around our brains at any one time. While we are wide-awake and focused on the day's tasks, our subconscious 'stupid' filter stops any thoughts except for those that are tried-and-tested. The net result is a less creative self and the effect of a less active brain.

But when we are relaxed, distracted and/or tired, the subconscious and the 'stupid' filter are also lulled into a more sedate mode. Once this happens, many more of those millions of bouncing thoughts are able to reach the conscious mind. The moment they reach the conscious (or that moment of realization) is the critical moment for creative thought capture. Sometimes, the active conscious and 'stupid' filter will kick back in too fast and the thought will be lost (at least for the

> Millions of diverse and disparate thoughts, notions and ideas are bouncing around our brains at any one time.

time being). At other times, the idea will register with the conscious before the filter can re-engage. When this happens we are actually able to 'remember' the thought/idea/notion.

Are you ready to capture this new-found idea? Do you have an idea journal and pen? Are you ready to scribble down the thought for later evaluation? If you are in the shower, do you have a waterproof pad and pencil to hand? Is your phone nearby so that you could quickly send yourself an email, explaining the thought you have had. This great thought that fought so hard to make it to your conscious is in jeopardy of being lost if you don't capture it quickly. Whatever you do, do not try to decide simply to remember it for later. By not taking the opportunity to record this notion immediately, you are likely to lose it forever; it will be quickly forgotten and probably never retrieved from the recesses of the mind. By placing the idea back in your head, the 'stupid' filter has another chance to render it impotent and leave the idea quickly forgotten. Write it down, capture it and with utmost speed! Boom-boom!

Key Takeaways:

1) Counterintuitively, our brain is more active when the rest of the body isn't focused and wide-awake.

2) Immediately capturing any new ideas/thoughts/notions allows for later capitalization and/or refinement at a later time.

3) Don't try to remember without recording these new ideas – don't give the 'stupid' filter another chance to repress that idea.

IDEA
SELECTION
PHASE

So now that we've explored our Nifty Nine creative principles and our brains are generating oodles of ideas, notions and creative thoughts, what do we do with them all?

It isn't unusual for one of our typical workshops to generate more than 1,000 new ideas. Obviously, we cannot reasonably pursue 1,000 ideas, even if all of them happened to be unique without duplicates and even if time and resources were not limiting factors. Since time and resources are always limiting factors, a process for selecting ideas must be implemented to maximize the idea-generation process.

In fact, how we select from ideas, as individuals and organizations, is the subject of much study. James E Schrager, clinical professor of entrepreneurship and strategy at the University of Chicago: Booth School of Business, is at the forefront of applying this behavioral strategy to the corporate world. He relates this concept to learning how to play a woodwind musical instrument (i.e. oboe). The mechanisms for playing the oboe are quite simple, you blow into one end, then move fingers across the holes on top and varying sounds come out the other end. However, to play it well, the right holes must be covered and uncovered at the right times. And while practice is critical to gaining expertise, the true expert understands how to adjust the fingers based on the outflow sound. In essence, what the player is actively doing is recognizing that the raw data is a representation from which patterns could be identified and acted upon.

Whenever we need to select from a disparate, and often voluminous, quantity of data, representation allows us to identify the key and critical questions and, from there, formulate a course of action. As a pilot, I am constantly receiving streams of data and using representation of this data to identify critical questions, answer them, and then act on them. It is important to mention that, while representations are a critical component of decision making, they do not provide solutions by themselves. However, once patterns have been recognized from the representations, the solutions emerge. We will look at some of these pilot applications and examples later in the book.

Representation and the corporate application of them is not a simple or quick matter, but by acknowledging the underlying process for our decision making, we can better position ourselves to sort through the ideas and, ultimately, to select the best ones to pursue.

In a recent conversation with James Vrtis, chief technical officer (CTO) for Truckstop Group, LLC (a leading provider of transportation technology), we discussed how his company selects from an over-active pipeline of potential projects (at times, 300-plus). Truckstop aims to provide seamless solutions across the entire supply chain, so every new project is first plotted on its appropriate location within the chain. The next step is weighing strategic options against existing product, as well as a modified SWOT (strengths, weaknesses, opportunities, threats) assessment to identify market solution gaps currently existing in supply chain solutions.

The key, according to James, is keeping the audience in the market. The critical question asked in evaluating a potential new project is, "What is the size of the market and are they reachable in our market place?"

By answering these questions, James and the Truckstop executive team are then able to answer the 'build or park' question. If the answer is "build"', then the next question is "build ourselves or partner out?" Both have pros and cons that must then be evaluated further. For example, a partnership will improve speed to market but might sacrifice the capturing of all necessary data. However, a 'build ourselves' mentality will cost time and resources but would be customizable to capture all data and meet all required parameters. By following this process, each project is evaluated with a critical eye towards true solutions that provide value and are sustainable.

> ## A selection process that allows bias creep will undermine all the idea-generation efforts.

A strong word of caution: A selection process that allows bias creep will undermine all the idea-generation efforts. I've frequently observed idea-generation processes that take great effort to engage everyone and accurately record all of the generated ideas only to be subverted by selection phase bias.

What is bias? Bias is simply the aggregate of our collective experiences, thoughts and actions. It can be positive, neutral or negative, but it poses a formidable barrier to both creative thought and, more importantly, idea selection. However, our previous understanding of representation and its resulting critical questions do not fall into this definition of bias.

Why does bias creep happen, especially after all the effort expended in the idea selection phase? A closer look at the typical company's organization and culture will provide a likely answer.

Virtually every company has a hierarchical scheme with various levels of management ultimately leading to the executive suite. This is true even in companies that boast of a 'flat' management structure. In reality, there is no such thing as a truly 'flat' management structure and for good reason. Not everyone can make the hard decisions necessary to establish, maintain and grow an organization. If everyone had an equal vote and voice, decisions would be made mostly based on popularity regardless of better ideas generated. Another alternative scenario would be no decisions being made due to the ensuing gridlock of competing ideas.

Clearly, there must be an established rank and order to allow for smoother work flows and for expeditious decision making. This is even true in more progressive companies that allow anyone to generate, and sometimes even pursue, ideas. Typically, these companies will refer to their workers as 'team members' and 'associates' to convey a unified sense of purpose. Semantics aside, these organizations also have rank and order, even if it's not obviously clear from titles.

Since there is a rank and order, when an idea is generated, it will typically be evaluated by one or more people who will give immediate consideration to the idea based on their understanding of the issues and/or likelihood of gaining higher approval. There can be no question that unintentional (and in some cases, intentional) bias is employed in these evaluations. Once bias is introduced into the process, it becomes very difficult to make a decision that counteracts this bias, especially if the decision entails higher management approval.

We've previously talked about a skilled, unbiased moderator being one option for facilitating idea selection, but there are other methods as well. Regardless of the type of organization, there must be practical processes used to winnow down and select from all the ideas flowing from the now-full idea pipeline. This is especially important at times when resources are finite and very limited.

These methods can be used independently or in conjunction with one another. The key is that they help minimize, and possibly eliminate, popularity and rank bias in the idea-selection phase. But even more importantly, they allow for collective agreement and the formation of a broader support base to help propel the idea(s) through the 'Change' and 'Innovation' phases.

MULTI-VOTING

As a Chicago native, I take a lot of good-natured ribbing regarding the city's politics and voting. I hear this one quite often, "Vote early, vote often, and don't let being dead stop you". We have certainly had our share of political shenanigans but there is something that can be learned from all of this when it comes to idea selection; multiple voting.

Let's say that the idea selection group is comprised of ten people drawn from different ranks and functionalities within the company. This selection group is now tasked with selecting from a list of 100 possible ideas. To achieve the task, every member of the group is given ten votes with the only rule being that they can't vote for any single idea more than five times. To protect anonymity and to mitigate any possible bias creep, it is best if each selection group member has all of the ideas listed on sheets of regular paper stapled together. There should be one idea per line, with a space for the tick-marked votes.

Each member of the group can vote based on their own individual notions of what makes for a pursuable idea. There should be absolutely no coercion or convincing regarding the criteria for voting. Ideally, the person presenting and tabulating the votes should be unbiased and separate from the voting process itself. Also, there can be no identifying information attached to any of the ideas up for consideration. The votes should be based solely on the ideas themselves and their potential merits.

After all of the votes are in and tabulated, the ten ideas with the highest number of votes are put up for the next round of voting. All of the rules are the same except that each person has fewer total votes and there is the caveat that individuals must not vote more than three times for any single idea.

From this round, there should emerge a few clear 'winning ideas' selected with the full participation and agreement of the selection group and without bias creep. These ideas can now be presented to the group together (rather than individually) for discussion and debate.

Previously, we wanted to ensure that no critical thought or negativity would be introduced into the idea generation phase. After all, we wanted to make sure that we were able to harvest every possible idea without dissuading anyone from offering any idea. Now, we must be able to look critically at the selected ideas. Are the ideas plausible? Realistic? Likely to be approved? What capital (if any) requirements might be necessary to move any of the selected ideas forward?

During this critical review process, other new ideas might be generated as offspring of the debate. As long as the process is allowed to continue without personal attacks, these new ideas can be considered and evaluated immediately. Critical thought and debate are crucial to refining and moving ideas forward from the 'Idea' phase to the 'Change' phase and hopefully leading to true 'Innovation'.

Critical thought and debate are crucial to refining and moving ideas forward from the 'Idea' phase to the 'Change' phase and hopefully leading to true 'Innovation'.

Another benefit of the critical evaluation process taking place after the multi-voting: It's unlikely that the ideas remaining were actually offered up by any of the participants of the selection group. This allows for members of the group to advocate or evaluate the selected ideas without personal bias or emotional attachment. In essence, everyone in the group becomes both an actual advocate and a 'devil's advocate' for the ideas. The net result: a collectively selected group of ideas that have been refined through the critical review process. And since these ideas were selected and reviewed collectively, they are much more likely to garner a broader support base which will be very valuable in the 'Change' phase.

Key Takeaways:
1) Multi-voting allows for a democratic narrowing of a master ideas list through everyone's participation in an unbiased manner.
2) Once narrowed down, personal bias is likely not in play as everyone can actively debate and critically evaluate the remaining ideas.

THE BUCKET LIST

There is another method via which the idea selection group could winnow down the master list of ideas to a workable few; the bucket method. Ahead of the idea-selection meeting, the group can decide on the buckets or categories in which each idea might be best placed. For instance, these buckets could include 'good ideas', 'possible ideas', 'not practical', 'not possible' and 'other'. Within the 'good' and 'possible' idea buckets, there could be further categorization to include 'minimal capital', 'capital intensive' and 'other'.

The key point is that all of the buckets should be defined and agreed upon ahead of the idea-selection meeting. It's also important to make certain that there is a bucket for 'other'. This allows for placement of ideas where there is considerable disagreement as to the proper categorization of a particular idea or where an idea simply does not fit into any of the other buckets.

The process starts with each idea being presented to the group either verbally by a skilled and unbiased meeting leader, or in writing. Each idea is then subject to critical evaluation and analysis as to its proper categorization. Categorization of many ideas will be fairly obvious; others won't be quite as clear.

Once all of the ideas have been placed into their respective buckets, a closer look is given to the ideas in the 'other' bucket. This evaluation should be conducted with the aim of finding any other potential 'good' or 'possible' ideas. If the dis-

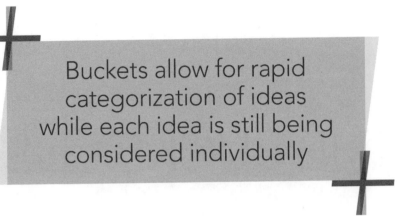

Buckets allow for rapid categorization of ideas while each idea is still being considered individually

agreement is regarding placement in any of the other buckets, there need not be any further debate. Either way, these ideas should not, at this time, be given further consideration. If the debate cannot resolve the disagreement, a silent vote should be taken as to its final placement.

Ideas not being considered at this time (within the multi-voting method or bucket method) should not be simply thrown away. Often an idea is simply not ready for the current environment, but may be ready at some time in the future. All recorded ideas that have not been selected should be on the recurring idea timetable for future consideration. This timetable can be set for one year on, five years on, ten years on, or whatever best suits the organization's parameters. At that time, all non-selected ideas from the past should be added to the new ideas up for consideration. This allows not only for a database of ideas, but for a previously non-selected idea to be that next great idea in the future.

With the remaining 'good' and 'possible' ideas, the next step of categorization can now be taken. Each idea can be evaluated regarding its likely capital requirements. While ideally, ideas should be selected without consideration of capital requirements, the reality is quite different. For all ideas in the 'capital intensive' buckets, the selectors must understand the nature of what is required to move them forward, including business cases, charters, senior management approval, perhaps even board-level approval. This shouldn't necessarily preclude these ideas from being selected, but they do need to be identified at this point.

This is especially relevant to organizations facing fiscal issues that cannot easily afford a 'capital intensive' idea but would be willing to consider and implement 'minimal capital' ideas. With the successful implementation and benefits received from these 'minimal capital' ideas, a foundation for ideation will be established and allow for greater risk taking in the future. But even for those organizations willing to invest in a 'capital intensive' idea, it remains critical that idea selectors understand what they are proposing to consider and implement.

Once all the ideas have been placed in their respective sub-buckets (capital requirements), they can now be debated individually and critically evaluated, or subject to a round of multi-voting to narrow down the list.

Key Takeaways:
1) Buckets allow for rapid categorization of ideas while each idea is still being considered individually.
2) Sub-buckets (capital requirements) allow for upfront acknowledgment of capital intensive ideas and their respective workloads.
3) Buckets can be combined with multi-voting to narrow down the final list of to-be-considered ideas.

CHANGE

"What if we don't change at all ...
and something magical just happens?"

Through our idea selection process, we have our chosen few ideas to pursue. Now, we need to move to the next step in our systemized ideation (Ideas + Change = Innovation). Like many processes, 'Change' has its own methodology or logistics as well.

When we think logistics, we usually conjure up images of trucks, warehouses, freight trains and the like. Many people consider logistics to be a tactical operation in the overall supply management of an organization and they would be correct, at least in their pragmatic definition. In fact, numerous trade publications use the word 'logistics' (i.e., "Inbound Logistics", "Logistics Management") referring to different aspects in supply chain management.

However, if we take a closer look, logistics is simply the methodology for accomplishing a task. It doesn't require a mode of transportation or storage but it does require a process. In effect, the trade publications mentioned above are really touting best process practices as it pertains to various supply chain tactics. By practical definition, logistics equals processes; thus logistics is both prevalent and relevant in all organizations and even in our personal lives. It answers the critical question, how do we get from here to there? Or how do we accomplish what we seek to accomplish?

In a recent discussion with John P Surma, deputy chair of The Federal Reserve Bank of Cleveland, board member at Marathon Petroleum and Ingersoll Rand and former chairman and CEO of United States Steel Corporation (US Steel), John quickly summarized the key component of any (change) initiative: "It's all about leadership – the ability to articulate and then implement a vision together."

John mentioned what had happened while he was at Marathon Oil during a period of transition from a strong, long-serving CEO who was nearing retirement. While they were successful in making the change, there was a gap in the overall leadership and direction of the company. As a result, the company stalled until new strong leadership was established. In this case, the succession vision wasn't clearly articulated, leading to a general lack of direction.

Conversely, in 2002-2003, when John became president of US Steel, he was not satisfied with the feel, culture and management style in place. After much consideration, and despite the skepticism of others, John embarked on a platform of employee safety. Employee safety would be the first thing talked about in all board meetings and reports. Despite initial resistance, and through the use of creative incentives, this resistance was broken down and became universally accepted. As a result of John's strong leadership and clearly articulated vision, employee safety not only greatly improved but became a springboard for other organizational initiatives.

He further talked about the critical steps to successful change (not necessarily in order of importance):

- Leaders must recognize what success looks like. They must know what/when they've succeeded with the goals of the initiative. It must be something that everyone can see and mostly agree upon and this something must be able to be reasonably and simply articulated.
- The project or change team must be diverse in thought, background, demeanor, authority, gender, and so on. Without this diversity, the ability to be successful is greatly hindered.
- Structure, plan, timeline, milestones, responsibilities, and so on, must be accounted for and recorded to help guide the initiative. It could be in the form of a project charter or be something less formal, but either way it must be present.
- "Tell the truth all the time." Honest communication is the ultimate weapon for combating resistance and successfully pushing forward change initiatives.

As a further example of everyday logistics in action, consider a person planning to purchase a new vehicle. It is unlikely that he will walk into the first dealership he encounters and purchase the first vehicle he sees. Instead, he will consider the type of vehicle he needs or wants and follow this with research into different vehicles that meet those requirements. After ascertaining dealer pricing, he will probably research his credit score (if financing) and his borrowing rate of interest. Next, he will test-drive the different vehicles, followed by negotiating pricing and terms with different dealers. Finally, he will agree on the price with the winning dealer and drive off into the sunset with his new vehicle.

Each of these steps comprises the logistics of purchasing a vehicle. There are corresponding logistics involved with the dealer receiving the car from the manufacturer and around the internal steps, including marketing, licensing, plating, reordering, commissions and so on.

We can illustrate the above scenario more coherently using flow charts, where each event creates a decision tree leading to additional questions and answers. Usually, everything we do has a process. Consider all the steps and decision making normally employed with going to work in the morning. Starting with waking up, we proceed through our normal routine allowing for flexible responses to the day's events. For instance, did we actually get out of bed on time? If yes, then we continue through the routine as usual. If no, we might ascertain how far behind schedule we are. If only a few minutes, we might cut short part of the routine. If considerably behind, we might even skip steps in our quest to arrive at work on time. Which steps are skipped and/or truncated depends on the relative priority of each of those steps. In fact, if some of those steps are higher priorities than being on time, you won't skip those steps at all and will accept the fact that you'll arrive at work late.

Most of the time we don't consciously think about the process, but it is there and employed constantly. We can legitimately refer to this process as the logistics of arriving at work on time. If we really wanted to analyze everything we normally do in a given day, we will undoubtedly discover many different processes and sub-processes that help us achieve our desired results. We are, in effect, our own logistics machines, putting into action the processes and decisions to achieve our desired results.

Similarly whenever we change our routine or are forced to change part of our routine, we use some sort of process to guide us. And we also need this process to guide us when moving forward with our previously selected ideas. This process could be informal and largely based on personal experience or it could be something that is

> Since most of us don't do everything exactly the same way every day, we employ processes to direct and guide us through those differences or changes. Thus, Changistics is a critical part of our every day, albeit occasionally subconsciously.

given considerable thought and planning. Either way, this process (change logistics) guides us through the change. To simplify, I invented the term "Changistics" to describe the process (or logistics) involved with any change. Since most of us don't do everything exactly the same way every day, we employ processes to direct and guide us through those differences or changes. Thus, Changistics is a critical part of our every day, albeit occasionally subconsciously.

However, for Changistics to maximize its success potential, especially when confronted with unplanned obstacles, we need to understand the three components that comprise Changistics: Plan, Communicate and Execute. Within these components, there are many key takeaways and concepts that will help us maximize our successful Changistics journey.

Key Takeaway(s):
1) Change is like any other process, in that there is a particular logistics or method to moving forward.
2) Changistics is the logistics of better change.
3) The three critical building blocks of Changistics are Plan, Communicate and Execute.
4) These building blocks overlap and are not mutually exclusive.

PLAN

CHANGISTICS TAKEAWAY #1: BE THE PILOT IN COMMAND. ALWAYS CONTINUE TO FLY YOUR PLANE.

Ask yourself this question: Do events control you or do you control events? Or better yet, are you influenced by life events or do you influence life events? How many times are we faced with a situation that seems hopeless and resign ourselves to whatever fate dictates?

Resignation is insidious. Sometimes when 'the chips are down', we will set aside our own free will and ability to take charge of the situation and instead wallow in whatever has been presented to us. Typically, this will happen at a 'failure moment'. For many of us, the failure is a *fait accompli*. We think, "it is time to accept the reality and finality and move on". But if we look at the failure not as an end in itself but as a means to an end, then the failure is just a speed bump to be traversed and not finality. In fact, failure might not be a bad thing. Failure can spur us to be more innovative, better at what we do and possibly reach an even better solution than originally intended. The key is not to resign and/or give up when confronted with failure. After all, failure is an opportunity to improve if we alter our mindset to accept it as an impetus for being better.

As a professional pilot, I meticulously plan my flights including giving strong and continuous consideration to the weather and planning for it. I cannot control the weather, but I can control how I react to it, including choosing to divert the plane during particular conditions, or not fly in these conditions at all. However, there are times when, despite my extensive planning, Mother Nature has surprises up her sleeve. Regardless, as Pilot in Command (PIC), I must continue to fly the plane safely, even if that means landing at an alternate location. And as previously mentioned, there is an old pilot's saying that a successful flight concludes with a safe landing and if it happens to be at the intended destination, then it's a bonus.

In fact, redefining failures is one of the continuing struggles through which we can make general aviation safer. As pilots, we are mission-orientated; in other words, our goal, perhaps our reason for being a pilot, is to complete the mission. We will then define the mission as flying from our origin (point A) to our intended destination (point B). But many pilots have a tendency to miss one key part of any mission: safety. They become so focused on the mission, they ignore warning signs and push on regardless. Unfortunately, this has led to many preventable accidents. In fact, not only do these accident pilots fail at the real mission, landing safely, they ultimately fail at their intended mission, getting from A to B. Success in a flight is a safe landing. It is not, and should not, be considered a failure if that landing is back at the original airport or at an alternate airport.

It is no different with life's surprises for any of us. Sometimes, we can anticipate them and pre-empt either the change itself or its impacts. At other times, we may not be able to control the events themselves, but we can certainly control how we react to them and our subsequent actions. If we are able to redefine the word 'failure' to mean something more reflective and to reflect an 'opportunity', we will have the ability to learn from it and become even better.

Consider this scenario (an actual event from before I became a pilot):

> *As a consultant, I am frequently travelling last minute to various client loca-tions. Sometimes, I can travel by car; other times, I am forced to rely on the airlines and their pre-set schedules. As people who travel from smaller cities can readily attest, the available schedules are frequently less than desirable.*

> *One fine morning, I was on a 5:45am flight to a hub city and connecting from there to my destination city. That first flight was the only flight I could take that would give me enough time at the client's location. When I woke up that morning at 4:30am, it was raining heavily with thunderstorms in the area. I received an email from the airline (identity withheld to protect the guilty) clearly and unambiguously stating that the flight was cancelled. I immediately emailed my client to notify them of my non-arrival and re-scheduled for the following day. I then went back to sleep with the intention of rescheduling the flight for the following day when I awoke.*

> *At 8:00am, when I contacted the airline to reschedule, I was informed that the flight had not been cancelled and had actually departed, albeit with a 90-minute delay time. As a result, if I wished to reschedule, it would cost me an additional $250. When I conveyed to them that I had written notice from them about the cancellation, they disavowed responsibility for it. Es-sentially, I was out of luck.*

> *Unsatisfied with that response, I escalated the situation all the way to a vice president, who informed me that since the flight actually departed, they were in no way responsible for rescheduling my flight without the addition-al fee. When I offered to send him the email notice, he claimed the email was from a third party (even though it said it was from the airline itself, complete with the logo) and they would take no responsibility. It was yet an-other shining example of abysmal customer service and lack of responsibility. (Had I thought better of it, perhaps a Twitter shout-at would have brought me the desired resolution, but I was not, at that point, initiated into the Twitter-verse.)*

*I ended up driving to Chicago the following day and booking a direct flight
to the destination city on another airline. I have never flown again with the
original airline following that day's events.*

At first, I was quite angry. How could the airline not take responsibility for
its own screw-up? Why should I have had to pay extra just to get them to
rectify their own error? Why did I now have to placate my client about my
non-arrival, even though it wasn't my fault? What was I going to do about this
in the future?

Conventional thinking would have classified this as three failures, with the second directly caused by the first. First, the airline failed to notify me properly
regarding the status of my flight. Second, the airline's notification failure directly
caused me to fail to reach my client that day. Third, the airline's refusal to take
rightful responsibility lead me to shun that airline in future. Was this, then, a
total failure or a setback that would lead to greater opportunity?

After my initial anger had subsided and calmer thinking prevailed, I decided
to do something about it. I had always wanted to be a pilot and fly myself to
different places; in fact, 20 years ago, I had intended to take flying lessons but
somehow life had got in the way (or rather, I had allowed it to get in the way and
to distract me from my goal). Ten years ago, I had intended to take flight lessons,
but again life got in the way. Now, I was ready to do it so that I did not have to
rely exclusively on the commercial airlines for my distant business and personal
travel. I refused to allow events beyond my control to affect my future course of
action. Instead, I took control.

To make my goal a reality, I needed to plan appropriately. I understood that,
with each level of certification, there would be a corresponding time investment.
This time would involve preparing for the written test, reviewing other material
on the ground ahead of training flights and spending time reviewing the flights
after they were completed. There also would be a time investment in the training
flights and in the preparation and execution of the practical test.

To find out just how much time this would require, I spoke to many different
pilots, researched pilot information websites and other online resources. This research enabled me to identify the likely timescale involved. If I pursued my goal
aggressively, it would take less time and money. If I was more laid-back about it,
it would take more of both.

I also needed to plan for the requisite costs, including written materials, various pilot supplies (charts, headsets and so on), flight instructor fees and plane rental fees. Through my research, I discovered that by pushing ahead with this quickly, I would spend less money on both the flight instructor and plane rental, as each new lesson would require less of a review.

Finally, I had to plan for the intangibles such as the impact on my family. My wife doesn't like small-airplane flying and would have preferred me not to become a pilot, despite the incredible advantages it presents. While I did not initially handle this well, I didn't perceive her reaction as being fatal to the overall goal. I hoped that, eventually, she would understand and also recognize the benefits. (For example, my kids have enjoyed the benefits of being flown around, especially on short-flights to Chicago to visit their grandparents.) Meanwhile, I planned to find a way of taking up flying without upsetting my wife (too much). To her credit, she has been incredibly gracious about the matter, despite her ongoing discomfort.

Via considerable effort and dedication to learning, practicing and flying nearly every day, I was able to gain the various certifications necessary not to only fly a plane in good weather, but even in poor-visibility weather and to fly others professionally as well. As a professional pilot, I have additional income streams available to me, by working as a corporate pilot for local companies. I had been able to take an adverse experience (or failure) and channel it into positive action. I was not, and am not, willing to bow down and play the victim. I refused to believe in "it is what it is". I will only believe that "it is what you make of it". I refused to take what the airline gave me (nothing!). I chose to make the airline's failure into an opportunity to take matters into my own hands. I turned failure into opportunity and haven't looked back since.

We are constantly faced with changes in our everyday lives. Some of them are (or can be) reasonably anticipated and perhaps planned for. Others are sudden and/or involuntary. Either way, the only constant in life is change. How we plan and react to change is critical to personal success and the realization of our goals.

It is too easy and convenient simply to blame others for our lack of success. We blame society for all of its ills. We blame our governments for their ineptness (even though it was us who elected them). With all the blaming and pointing fingers, we ultimately concede control of our own destinies, taking ourselves out of our optimal state and moving instead to the United States of Denial.

How we plan and react to change is critical to personal success and the realization of our goals.

Denial is a powerful psychological weapon that we employ to ward off the truth. With apologies to Jack Nicholson (*A Few Good Men, Columbia Pictures, 1992*), we can't (and don't want to) handle the truth. It is easier to close our eyes, ears, and brains and pretend that whatever ails us is not our fault. And it is therefore acceptable to blame a convenient culprit. We see what we want to see and believe what we want to believe, regardless of the reality or the truth. But we can, and should, handle the truth. How else will we improve? How else will we make ourselves and the world around us better if we won't even concede that it is our problem to solve?

It is all about responsibility and accountability. We are responsible and accountable for our own actions. While other people and events can influence our decision making and actions, ultimately, it falls to us to move ourselves forward. Air Traffic Control (ATC) can give us new and unexpected routings, the weather can suddenly turn ugly, the plane can start running a bit rough, and it still doesn't matter. We are in control of our planes and our destinies. We must continue to pilot them to safe landings. If we don't, the results and consequences are on us.

It would have been too easy for me simply to blame the airline and leave it at that. But what guarantee would I have had that it wouldn't happen again? I refused to be a victim and took concrete action that would reduce the likelihood of a repeat occurrence. This action required an investment of time, effort and money, as does every change worth implementing, but it would be difficult to argue that a solid return wasn't achieved for those investments.

> We are in control of our planes and our destinies. We must continue to pilot them to safe landings. If we don't, the results and consequences are on us.

I covered personal returns on investment (PROI) in my previous book (*Selfish Altruism – Managing & Executing Successful Change Initiatives*, Booklocker 2012), but perhaps a quick refresher is in order.

Every initiative, whether organizational or personal, requires investments of different sorts. With a purely financial investment, the investor will require a certain ROI. After all, the financial investment didn't need to go to this initiative and could have been invested elsewhere.

There is also another type of investment present with virtually all initiatives; personal investments. Every initiative, whether it is pursuing a selected idea, moving forward with a new system or process or even a personal project (such as losing weight), requires non-financial personal investments; namely time, effort and emotion. Like their financial investment cousins, they also require a return or PROI.

This PROI does not need to be financial, but it does have to be sufficient to provide either an extrinsic or intrinsic motivation to invest personal resources. Examples of non-financial PROI include promotion opportunities, recognition as a subject matter expert, sense of fulfillment, being part of a winning team, opportunities to be part of and/or lead future projects, and so on.

In an interview with John Correnti, CEO of Big River Steel (and former CEO of Birmingham Steel and Nucor), he mentioned that, while there are other motivators, green (money) is still the most effective. Through utilization of productivity-based cash incentives, paid out weekly, he receives both higher volume and higher-quality tons produced each week. For example, consider a great week, where a worker brings home $800 base ($20/hour) plus an additional $1,200 in incentives, making a total of $2,000. The following week, he brings home a check of only $1,200 (base plus $400 in incentives). His wife immediately notices the difference. Does she care that the manufacturing process broke down or about the other reasons for the reduced pay? While she might understand the concept, ultimately, she will strongly urge her husband to figure out what has gone wrong and get back to earning a higher wage. That worker is now doubly motivated not to let history repeat itself, if for no other reason than to re-earn the incentives and not disappoint his wife.

Of course, John offers non-financial incentives that also help achieve higher rates of productivity, such as encouraging an inclusive mentality whereby

> Our intended goals should not be set back by a strong crosswind, a bump in the road, or even turbulence

everyone works (and gets their hands dirty). There are no job descriptions (job descriptions tend to limit workers to what they will or will not do), and he has developed a culture in which everybody talks to everybody else. John walks the shop floor every day to help people do their jobs and provides the right equipment in the right hands. There is no clocking in or out as there is a culture of trust, and everyone is treated with dignity and respect. All of these serve as ready examples of PROI in action. When we deliver on PROI by providing these personal returns, we receive back a highly energized and motivated team, capable of achieving, and inspired to do, greater things.

John tells a story regarding a caster he bought from Germany for one of his plants in 1980. At some point after the purchase and installation, the sellers inquired if the machine was producing 100 tons per hour. John's reply was that it was producing 140 tons per hour. The sellers were incredulous and skeptical, so they travelled to the plant to see it in action. They immediately noticed the motors were double horsepower compared to the original one, that the piping allowed double the flow and the machine was operating with an efficiency for which it was never designed for (and yet was now producing). As a result of John's delivery of PROI, his staff were inspired and motivated which drove forward efficiency and production. They felt encouraged to recommend and make changes that benefitted both the company and themselves.

Suffice to say, without a return on personal investments of time, effort and emotion, we would be less likely to undertake any sort of pain to effectuate a change. After all, who likes to feel pain, especially if there is nothing to be gained from it? And like any investment, we expect a certain return. It is this return that allows us to undertake the pain of a personal investment, and as long as we start realizing this return, we will stay motivated and on-track.

What happens when we inevitably hit that 'bump in the road'? We must continue to fly our airplanes. When a pilot is on the final approach for landing, he positions the plane on the extended center line of the runway with no drift and pointing straight towards the runway, ready for landing. If he encounters a strong crosswind and doesn't take positive corrective action, the plane will drift in the direction the wind is blowing. The plane might not be pointing straight and, on landing, might actually go off the side of the runway, damaging the airplane and possibly resulting in injuries (or worse). By taking immediate corrective actions, such as crabbing, slipping, or even a go-around, to land on a different runway or at a different airport, the pilot affirms his or her control of the situation and allows for a positive and safe outcome.

Key Takeaways:
1) Our intended goals should not be set back by a strong crosswind, a bump in the road, or even turbulence.
2) We need to recognize the situation immediately and then take corrective action to stay on-track and continue to point straight down the successful goal achievement runway.
3) We are in command and we must stay in command to achieve positive results.
4) Always seek out PROI and then deliver on them to create and maintain a high level of engagement.

CHANGISTICS TAKEAWAY #2: REDEFINE FAILURE TO ENABLE LESSONS LEARNED.

Successful change management requires a process that, if planned, communicated and executed properly, will lead to enduring achievement of objectives. In essence, proper change logistics or Changistics is the key to success.

'Plan', 'Communicate' and 'Execute' are the three foundation blocks used to build any change initiative, for a personal or for an organizational change. To understand Changistics better, a deeper exploration of the foundation blocks, and how they interrelate, is required. All three foundation blocks – 'Plan'; 'Communicate' and 'Execute' are required, and all three are present within one another. As such, they overlap and are not mutually exclusive, so that there are communication and execution elements within planning, planning and execution elements within communication and planning and communication elements in the execution stage.

It's worth noting that, even within the most meticulously and comprehensively researched plan, there are always the inevitable setbacks, speed-bumps or even sometimes outright failure.

Earlier, we discussed redefining 'failure' as 'opportunity' – a means to an even greater end. However, we must differentiate between the types of failure. There are three types of failure: incompetence, insubordinate and initiative.

Incompetence failure is when a task or activity is not successfully accomplished owing entirely to the lack of requisite skill and/or talent necessary. We all have our various levels of competence and experience for differing tasks and activities. When we place ourselves in a position that exceeds the limits of these levels, we open ourselves up to incompetence failure. This would be akin to a casual weekend softball player being selected as substitute shortstop for a major league baseball team. With the likely negative fall-out, the incompetence factor would be on display for all to see. Furthermore, the general manager of the team would reveal his incompetence for signing the casual softball player and the manager would reveal his incompetence for putting that player on the field.

This also manifests itself in the entrepreneurial world. The founder frequently has a marketable idea and/or service and the passion to move the business forward. However, he might lack the skills or experience to run the business successfully. He might be lacking in critical business skills and understanding. If this person doesn't acquire these skills, or hire someone else who has them, he risks the business failing, great ideas notwithstanding. If the business does fail because of this lack of requisite skills, it would be considered an incompetence failure.

I speak (again) from personal experience on this one.

My first entrepreneurial experience was the founding of an expedited air freight delivery service. The company was founded on the premise of providing the final mile to expedited air freight forwarders. We initially started in two mid-size hub city airports (Charlotte, NC and Denver, CO) and attempted expansion to three others. While the premise was good, and appreciated by many people in the forwarding community, my ability to run a business effectively was marginal at best. While I thought I knew how to manage people and accounting, I realized I was in way over my head (and beyond my abilities). With better intuition, I would have hired the experienced people I needed. Instead, I plodded along resolute in my determination to make it work (once again recalling the juxtaposition of stubborn versus tenacious).

Unfortunately, I wasn't able to make the business work and had to close the doors only two years after opening. My inexperience and inability to react properly to my business inexperience was a classic example of incompetence failure.

The key component of this failure was not incompetence in the requisite business and management skills (basic accounting, HR, and so on), but that I failed to recognize and detect that I was lacking these critical business skills and couldn't learn them well enough, or quickly enough, to give my business the continuity needed to be a viable enterprise. After all none of us are experts in everything, but the dividing line between incompetence failure and not failing lies in detecting and recognizing the things at which we are not so good, and then doing something constructive to remedy that shortcoming (not so easy to do).

Insubordinate failure is when the requisite skills and talents are present, but are willfully not employed, resulting in a task failure. While there is nothing wrong with doing things differently, there is a proper time and place for it. If instructed by an employer or authority figure to do something in a particular way or at a particular time, the expectation is for the task to be completed as instructed (with emergencies being the possible exception). There are people who are always thinking of creative and innovative ways in which to accomplish tasks, but without the approval to do so, any resulting failure is insubordinate failure.

Unfortunately, even if we are successful while being insubordinate, many non-progressive organizations will penalize the party responsible, when the opposite should happen. Their thinking is that if the offender (even though they were successful) is rewarded, it will set a negative precedent for the rest of the organization and order will be lost, with people doing whatever they think is best, rather than what management thinks is best. The unfortunate part is that it's that mentality which separates progressive from non-progressive.

A progressive organization will allow significant freedoms to their employees as long as tasks are accomplished within established minimum parameters. If an employee wants to deviate from the norms and experiment, then he or she is given freedom to do so. If it leads to an innovative method or process, then that person and/or their department is rewarded. If it fails to achieve minimum results, that person is not penalized and the lessons learned are shared within the organization. Effectively, insubordination is rendered moot due to the freedoms given from the outset and to the organizational reactions to failures. In this kind of organization, change is part of the everyday process and leaves little to fear.

A non-progressive organization expects strict compliance with every aspect of the established methods and processes. Deviation is not allowable or permissible. Employees that deviate are subject to discipline. Success resulting from deviation or innovation is rarely rewarded, since innovation is solely the province of senior management. Ultimately, this is the hallmark of an organization that does

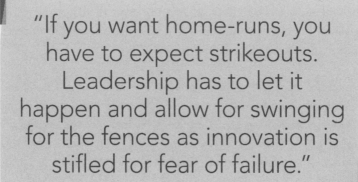

"If you want home-runs, you have to expect strikeouts. Leadership has to let it happen and allow for swinging for the fences as innovation is stifled for fear of failure."

things the way they have always done them and intends to do them this way for the foreseeable future. In this organization, change is something that is frowned upon and is rendered monstrous, leaving everything to fear.

Finally, we have initiative failure. Assuming approval has been given for experimentation and exploration, any resulting failure is the basis for greater learning and an ultimately more successful result. After all, experimentation and exploration, in approved and/or expected environments have led to all of the innovations we enjoy today. The keys to learning from failure are detection that a failure has occurred, the ability to identify and learn from lessons and pursuing a revised plan relatively quickly. As John Correnti is fond of relating from the career of Babe Ruth, arguably the greatest home-run hitter ever to play baseball, "If you want home-runs, you have to expect strikeouts. Leadership has to let it happen and allow for swinging for the fences as innovation is stifled for fear of failure."

Incompetence failure, if learned from, can be an effective building block for the future and shouldn't carry the full stigma of failure. However, insubordinate failure should only exist where an employee refuses to carry out a directive from management. In that case, it should carry the full stigma of failure in the hope that this type of failure can be mitigated, if not completely eliminated. Unfortunately, we frequently find that even initiative failure undeservedly carries the stigma of failure.

It is the rare change initiative that doesn't encounter a setback or two. Mostly, these setbacks, if properly planned for, can be mitigated and surmounted. But even when the setback is fatal to the change initiative, there is much learning that can be gleaned, but only if we are open to it. If we are open to the lessons learned, failure is truly transformed into opportunity.

> *Again, I speak from experience. After the release of my first book, Selfish Altruism, I employed the services of a PR firm to help spread the word and increase media exposure. A major component revolved around placement of articles and op-eds. A few months into the process, we jointly decided to tackle a current 'hot-button' issue through the prism of change management. The subject: gun control in the US. The timing: shortly after the Sandy Hook school shootings in Connecticut, which happened at the end of 2012.*

> *I wrote two articles that were picked up and featured in the Huffington Post (see Appendix B) and then republished by many other publications including those on both sides of the debate. My point was that no substantive change could be made until all sides had a meaningful and real place at the table. Also, no substantive change could be made until the root cause was unearthed and agreed upon. Had I left it there, the articles would have been more meaningful. However, I am not a believer in communicating a problem without presenting at least the beginning of a solution alongside it. At the urging of my publicist and the editor, I suggested a possible compromise solution at the end of the first article.*

> *I got blasted by both sides of the debate and through the carnage, my message was mostly lost. In the end, I broke one of my own rules while trying to keep another. I suggested a solution without having engaged both sides of the debate, which was ironic considering that was the very point and the impetus of the article.*

> *What I learned, besides having the temperature turned way up on hot-button issues, was that I should have stayed true to myself and the message I was trying to convey. Thankfully, there were those who, even after disagreeing with my suggestion, agreed on the premise of the article. My future publications communicated its salient points without deviating (but still allowing for active debate) and have been much more effective in conveyance.*

When a comprehensive plan is researched, conceived and executed, subsequent stage failures are also planned for and responded to accordingly. Part of this plan may be to re-examine critical parts of the process. Through this re-examination, a better way should prevail. In this regard, the failure has actually been planned for and should not result in anything more than a temporary setback.

Key Takeaways:

1) In most cases, failure should not be an ending, but rather a speed-bump.

2) If we (or our organizations) allow it, our finished product will be directly and positively influenced by the lessons learned from these speed-bumps.

3) We must always be looking for learning opportunities even when facing a big speed-bump (including the untimely demise of a project).

CHANGISTICS TAKEAWAY #3: FAILURE TO PLAN IS PLANNING TO FAIL.

Unfortunately, there are times when we don't put forth a comprehensive plan or we don't do the appropriate research. The result is a fourth type of failure: planning failure. While an argument can be made that this type of failure is really a sub-set of incompetence failure, it is deservedly its own category. After all, a person engaging in a change initiative may indeed be competent and follow established and expected procedure, but still ultimately fail through lack of appropriate planning.

In fact, almost all change initiative failures can ultimately be traced back to the planning stage. Thus, the planning stage in the timeline of a change initiative is the change initiative's most pivotal building block. We all celebrate when a plan 'comes together', but do we truly understand everything that goes into its successful culmination?

Planning starts with a detailed look into the circumstances potentially necessitating the change. Typically, when we encounter a roadblock or issue, we believe we already have the solution. Nowhere is this truer than in the political arena where ulterior motives, non-public agendas and special interest groups collide to help form policy legislation. In the wake of a tragedy, the politicians rush to portray themselves as rapidly working towards a timely and responsive solution. What isn't communicated is that, more often than not, the solution has already been pre-divined and this then becomes the proposed solution. Unfortunately, emotion has not been separated from the analysis; a thorough examination has not been completed (or even started) and opposing views have not been given equal weight and consideration (if they were given any consideration at all). All the while, the mantra is "the public demands that we respond quickly".

Before we can address that issue, let's consider another: In the rush to address the issue and proclaim a proposed solution, has the issue been correctly identified? If the issue has not been properly identified, then any proposed solution is akin to 'throwing glop on the wall and observing what sticks'. While this appears to be a time-tested method for political policy statements, it certainly doesn't garner public confidence in the legislators proposing a solution, or its likely success. This disconnect becomes especially obvious with hot-button political issues.

Consider the recent US gun policy proposals: In the wake of the tragic school shootings in Connecticut, proposals were recommended by a presidential task force and then announced by the President, all in a very short timeframe. Gun policy is an intensely complex issue with the need to balance constitutional rights and public safety. It is unreasonable to expect the real issues to be properly determined in such a short space of time, let alone a solution put forward that is likely to be successful and enduring. Yet, a set of solutions was proposed in this short timescale, ostensibly to show the public that their elected officials were listening and responding. This exposes the first step in planning success, or in this case, planning failure. The real issue must be properly identified prior to undertaking any change initiative planning.

> In the rush to address the issue and proclaim a proposed solution, has the issue been correctly identified?

Of course, emergency situations require rapid responses. But even these responses are the result of a process that involves significant training and simulation exercises. This planning process undoubtedly answers the 'what if' questions with tangible and actionable responses. Without this planning and advance preparation, the rapid responses would encounter significant execution difficulties. The emergency responses to 9/11 included rapid action by first responders. While their dedication and professionalism are unquestioned, the lack of adequate planning for such a large-scale and unprecedented operation hampered the effectiveness of their response. This is in no way an indictment on these brave responders, but an attempt to highlight an example, albeit extreme, of the importance of issue identification. The planning never anticipated such a large-scale response, and as a result, the response became chaotic and less effective.

Switching perspectives allows us to look at a personal change initiative and the importance of issue identification. One of the most frequent and popular New Year's resolutions is to lose weight. In an effort to achieve this resolution, some people will join a gym, others will purchase home exercise equipment and others will seek simpler ways to be more active, such as walking to work. The intent and initial effort may indeed be sincere, but generally, the effort soon slackens and then stops completely. While in January, it's almost impossible to find a parking space close to the health club, in February the best spaces are almost always available. What causes this distinct drop-off?

Resignation: This resignation will set in around achieving the resolution this year which ultimately dooms present execution of the plan. However, this failure doesn't impede the making of a future resolution. But does this future resolution stand a better chance of success when its creator so willingly relinquishes control? These initially determined people have stopped being the pilot in command and have instead conceded power to 'fate'. Simply put, not making a choice to be in command is still a choice, albeit a poor one.

While the simple view of this series of events is a failure in execution, it is really a failure in planning, leading to the inevitable failure in execution. The source of almost all execution failure is planning failure. In the case of the people resolved to lose weight, if we believed their failure to do so was only a matter of execution, then we could dismiss all explanations as excuses and look disapprovingly at their unwillingness to execute their resolutions. We might even consider it a refusal to execute it. We could (unfairly) ask, "why can't this person get it together? Isn't it important enough for him to get it done?"

Simply put, not making a choice to be in command is still a choice, albeit a poor one.

A better question would be: "What is the real issue present?" A closer look at the person is in order. While I do not rate most reality television, NBC's *The Biggest Loser* program, where overweight people compete to lose the most weight, seems to captivate me, despite the requisite drama. There is something inspirational about watching everyday people who have struggled to lose weight in the past reach their goals, while also tackling insidious issues such as a lack of self-confidence. Those who are less successful at tackling the insidious issues are also less successful at losing weight.

For the person struggling with their weight loss resolution, the real issue might not be the weight loss itself, rather something buried deeper. Consider an active person who, as he ages, suddenly finds himself weighing an extra 20 pounds. He has joined gyms in the past, only to give up at some point. When he started, he would be at the gym five days a week but this dropped off to three days, then once a week, then once a month and finally not at all. His excuses revolved around schedule conflicts, and then he simply said he didn't want to go. The extra weight remained. Was this a problem in execution or a problem in identifying the real problem? When we fail to identify the real problem, we are no closer to planning properly. And by not planning properly we are actually sabotaging the change itself. We will have indeed become our own worst enemy.

In the above case, the real problem was a lack of discipline and focus rooted in the lack of realization of a PROI. If this person wants to improve his discipline and focus, he will first need to realize a return on his investment in the weight

> And by not planning properly we are actually sabotaging the change itself. We will have indeed become our own worst enemy.

loss process. To achieve his goal, he will need to invest his time, effort, and emotion. He will need to understand fully what he is investing, how much he is investing and what the residual consequences of his investing will be.

Similar to any investment, he will expect a return on this investment. This return will be of a personal nature, such as looking and feeling better, not getting ill as often, having more energy, looking and feeling fitter and healthier, and of course, losing the actual weight.

While it's easy for me to simply say, "I will be focused, I will stay on task and I will achieve", it is easier to accomplish this if I am rewarded for my efforts, discipline and focus. As the returns aggregate, it will be easier to get up early to work out, easier to reduce empty-calorie eating, easier to make healthier choices and to continue the effort to lose weight.

In our quest to identify the real issue, emotion presents itself as a significant barrier. It doesn't matter whether the change is political (for example, gun policy), personal (weight loss) or organizational, emotion tends to muddy the waters of issue identification. The problem with emotion affecting issue exploration and ultimately, the change itself, is that it's a highly subjective and personal reaction to circumstances.

If we look at gun policy, depending on your personal viewpoints and beliefs, you will identify the real issue in a specific way and then fashion the solution based on that identification. Without taking sides, gun ownership groups might identify the problem as lax enforcement of current laws, mixed with the lack of legally armed citizens. Their solution might include rigid enforcement of current laws and for citizens to carry small arms legally. On the other hand, anti-gun groups will identify the real issue as a proliferation of semi-assault weaponry. Their solution might include restricting access to such weaponry and introducing a registry of existing owners/weapons. These are two very different solutions based on two very different real issue identifications. Both of these divergent issue identifications emanate from the very real emotional base of their respective populations.

The gun-control issue is an excellent example of emotion playing havoc with both the issue identification process and ultimately the decision-making process itself. Is it possible to completely eliminate emotion from either process? If not, is it possible to be emotion-neutral and to consider all sides and contributors to create an appropriate and enduring solution? Before answering these questions, consider the role of emotions in our more personal change initiative of weight loss.

If we now look at personal change such as weight loss, the impact of emotion on issue identification is also pronounced. Most people are highly sensitive about their appearance and weight. Those who are very overweight probably know that they are very overweight. It is an emotional and physical burden they carry. Is the real issue the excess weight or are there other issues that led to weight gain that are impeding a sustainable recovery?

Life presents us with an endless variety of changes. We have changes in our environment, changes involving loved ones and friends, geographical changes, physical changes, financial changes, career changes and many others. Many times the impact of these changes, either sudden or accumulative, will lead to emotional changes. We may seem to lack energy, we may want to be more comfortable, sleep more, eat more. Understanding what has changed emotionally, and why, will lead to identification of the underlying issue. At that point, we must begin by addressing the underlying issue and then plan to tackle the stated issue. If we only address the stated issue, or assume we know what the real issue is (without digging deeper), the planning will be missing critical steps and may well lead to an ineffective change or outright change failure.

Negative changes are worse than no changes at all. A bad change will involve the expenditure of significant resources, including money, time, effort and emotion. Worse, a negative change will require exponentially higher resources, first to undo the damage and then enact a positive change, but this time under duress. This is especially true if the real issue has not yet been identified. It's possible that no real change was necessary and that whatever spurred the action was due to an isolated incident. In this case, a bad change will cost dearly. But even in circumstances where no change will lead to gradual worsening, it is better to invest time in investigating and identifying the underlying issue rather than impetuously taking action that may be unwarranted or even harmful. This is akin to a patient suffering from some non-obvious malady. If the doctor doesn't make a careful diagnosis and prescribes the wrong medication, the patient will not improve and may well get worse.

When things start to go wrong, we react in one of two ways. The first is denial. We tell ourselves, "It really isn't a problem, it will go away by itself, it's just an

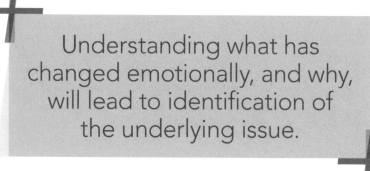

> Understanding what has changed emotionally, and why, will lead to identification of the underlying issue.

anomaly, it won't affect me or affect me much." Denial is one of the many built-in psychological self-defense mechanisms to sudden, adverse change. We may not even realize that we're in denial, but in every case, denial will not make the problem go away.

The second method is sudden reaction. We have come to terms with the fact that there is a problem and that it must be addressed swiftly. Certainly, we don't want the condition to deteriorate, so we make our best guess and attempt to rectify the issue. Most of the time, that impatience is unwarranted. More time and care could have been taken to estimate the nature of the problem, choose between options and then enact the change. The process doesn't have to be overly elongated, but it must take place.

As a pilot, I am trained in Aeronautical Decision Making (ADM). As with many other aspects of aviation, I've found (and continue to find) parallels between it and change management strategies and tactics. ADM comprises multiple processes and can be abbreviated using mnemonics. One of the processes for reacting to changing conditions is the DECIDE model. Each of these questions is actually a representation of the raw data received. These representations allow us to recognize patterns which lead us to appropriate solutions.

Detect:	Has something changed? If so, what has changed?
Estimate:	Does this change pose a risk? If so, what is the nature/severity of the risk?
Choose:	If I alleviate the change, what outcome do I desire?
Identify:	What actions should I take to facilitate the desired outcome?

Do: Take the actions that I have determined will lead to the desired outcome.

Evaluate: Have these actions produced the desired outcome?

Let's put this into action. Consider a short flight eastbound between South Bend, Indiana and Toledo, Ohio. With average wind conditions and a non-turbo-powered small single-piston plane, the trip time should be slightly less than 45 minutes at my filed altitude of 5,000 feet. After completing my preflight weather briefing and preparing the plane, I take off. Upon reaching and levelling off at 5,000 feet, the plane encounters unexpected light-to-moderate turbulence. Going through the DECIDE model:

(Detect):   I've detected a change from smooth flight to turbulent flight.

(Estimate):   This change doesn't pose a safety risk, but it is becoming increasingly uncomfortable.

(Choose):   I would like to get out of the turbulence and return to smooth (or relatively smooth flight).

(Identify):   I determine that if I change altitude, I would be likely to return to smooth flight. I could either go lower or higher. Lower probably won't reduce turbulence, so I choose a higher altitude.

(Do):   I contact Air Traffic Control (ATC) and request a higher new altitude (7,000 feet) on account of the turbulence. Upon receiving clearance, I climb to 7,000 feet and level off.

(Evaluate):   At 7,000 feet, the ride is much smoother, so the climb to 7,000 successfully alleviated the turbulence problem. If it hadn't smoothed out at 7,000, I would have returned back to 'Choose' and progressed through the steps again.

This model is easily transferable to any change, even personal changes. Once again, let's look at weight loss.

(Detect):   I've detected a change in my weight.

(Estimate):   If it's just a few pounds, maybe it isn't an immediate risk. But if it's more than a few, I definitely consider this an actionable risk.

(Choose):   I desire to return to a healthy weight for my age and height.

(Identify):   I determine that I will need to change my lifestyle to attain the desired healthy weight. This lifestyle will include both dietary and exercise components.

(Do):   I consult with a nutritionist for my dietary adjustments and decide to join a twice-weekly exercise class at the gym. I then follow the nutritionist's advice and regularly attend the exercise classes.

(Evaluate):   At appropriate intervals, I weigh myself. Have I started losing the excess weight? If yes, continue with current actions. If not, repeat the process starting from the 'Identify'.

Let's take a closer look at each of the individual elements that make up DECIDE.

DETECT

On the surface, detecting that a change has occurred should be relatively simple. If it is a personal issue, such as weight, we should be aware that our weight has changed and in which direction. Yet, recent surveys have shown that many overweight people don't consider themselves overweight. Furthermore, many parents of overweight children do not consider their children to be overweight. Undoubtedly, there is a social stigma attached to being overweight and many would rather deny the obvious than admit that there is a problem. In these cases, there is no detection of the change that has occurred. If a change is not detected, it cannot be successfully addressed.

In essence, detection is an exercise in scanning. How well are we scanning the signs for indications that something is changing? When we notice something is changing, do we immediately address it or shrug it off as not that important?

Consider an airplane flying in the clouds (instrument meteorological conditions) with no visual references other than the gray of the clouds.

To understand fully the nature of this potential disorientation, try this exercise: While standing up, have a friend place a colored pillowcase over your head, spin you around in a few circles and then suddenly stop the spinning. You can see, but do you know in which direction you are pointed? Do you know if you are going up or down? Your body will be telling you one thing but the reality will probably be very different). One cautionary note: Please make sure that your friend stays nearby – just in case.

If the pilot doesn't constantly scan his instruments looking for anomalies or other indications that airspeed, altitude and/or direction is changing, the situation can quickly spiral out of control with fatal consequences. His body might be telling him that the plane is banking or climbing and he will command the plane to correct, but the plane was flying straight. Now it's not flying straight, and worse, his corrections dangerously imperil its ability to continue safe flight.

Alternatively, the plane might be turning in one direction but the pilot's body is telling him that it's going straight, so no correction is made. Again, the consequences of the non-actions are potentially fatal. The pilot has to ignore what his body and eyes might be telling him and rely exclusively on his instruments.

But the pilot has to do more than detect the changes (if any), he needs to acknowledge the changes quickly and positively, assess the risks the changes present, decide on a course of action and then act on it, all in a very methodical and speedy fashion.

Lack of detection is so prevalent with social stigmas such as addictions that various recovery groups (such as Alcoholics Anonymous, Gamblers Anonymous) identify a person's admission that they have a problem as being their very first step towards recovery. If a person (or organization) sincerely wants to change, they have to admit (or self-detect) that they have a problem and that they need to change.

Returning to the person desiring to lose weight, he must first admit that the excess weight is a problem, that it's his problem, and that it needs to change. However, even though the excess weight is a problem, it might not be the real problem.

Key Takeaways:
1) Failure to plan is planning to fail.
2) While we cannot plan for every possibility, we can plan for categories of possibility.
3) Determining root causation is critical to planning.
4) Sometimes the issues we think are the problems, are not the real problems at all.
5) Use DECIDE as a tool to find the problem and then solve it

CHANGISTICS TAKEAWAY #4:
THE ISSUE PEOPLE IDENTIFY AS THE ISSUE IS USUALLY NOT THE REAL ISSUE.

Success in any change, and even more importantly, in any step of a change is largely dependent on identification of the real problem or issue. Often, the obvious problem is masking an obscured larger issue. This is true in both personal and organizational environments.

Within either environment, tough questions need to be asked and answered honestly to clear through the ambient fog. One of the more effective methods for successfully digging through the obscurations is through the (aforementioned) 5-Why method. The 5-Why method is the grown-up version of the over-inquisitive child. For instance, one of my children was upset that it was raining outside, preventing her from playing in the backyard. When I told her that rain is actually a good thing, she asked why. When I answered that it is a good thing because it gives the plants and trees a cool drink, I received another "why?" And so on, until my patience was exhausted and I distracted her with some books.

The 5-Why method works similarly. Consider again our overweight person. In a moment of clarity, he realizes and admits that, he is overweight, that it is a problem and that he owns both the problem and potential solution.

Q1:   "Why am I overweight?"
A1:   "Because I consume too many high-fat and high-calorie foods and do not exercise sufficiently."

Q2: "Why do I consume these foods?"
A2: "Because they provide ready comfort."

Q3: "Why do I need ready comfort?"
A3: "Because I am always tired and feel overworked."

Q4: "Why do I feel that way?"
A4: "Because I don't truly feel appreciated."

Q5: "Why don't I feel appreciated?"
A5: "I don't know."

While not an overly scientific method, the 5-Why method helps us get through the obscuration and shines a light on the real issue. In the above scenario, the real issue is likely to be a lack of self-worth and/or self-confidence. Further examination (probably by a professional) will unearth the events and/or feelings that evolved into the lack of self-worth/self-confidence. Even more importantly, it will help discover why those feelings are still impactful. Thus, the real issue is highlighted and can be addressed. Only after the real issue has been addressed, can successful change be realized.

The same process works in organizational change. For example, a division of a larger company is losing money.

Within either environment, tough questions need to be asked and answered honestly to clear through the ambient fog.

Q1:   "Why are we losing money?"
A1:   "Because we don't have a cohesive sales and marketing effort."

Q2:   "Why don't we have this effort?"
A2:   "We don't have the manpower and resources available."

Q3:   "Why don't we have the resources available?"
A3:   "We are on a tight budget that doesn't allow for these resources."

Q4:   "Why are we on such a tight budget?"

And so on.

While the organizational example may appear overly simplistic, the process does work. The 5-Why method doesn't have to stop with the five iterations of why; it is a suggested minimum with full flexibility to allow additional iterations as necessary. The 5-Why method is a proven tool in Total Quality Management (TQM) programs and is a solid technique for uncovering root issues, wherever they may occur.

Thus, the key lessons from the 5-Why method are 1) Keep digging deeper to uncover the real issue, 2) Don't attempt to solve the apparent problem with an answer to any of the why questions and 3) Make every effort to keep emotional responses out of the honest uncovering efforts.

Since 5-Why doesn't necessarily mean stopping with the fifth 'why?', when is the right time to stop digging? In other words, how do we know when we have reached the real issue to address?

If there remains an answer to a why question, then there is still buried treasure in the sand. When the only answer to a why question is "I don't know", then the real issue treasure will be exposed. At this point, the focus should shift from digging through the sand, to better understanding the newly uncovered issue.

For example, if the final why is preceded by a "because our CEO ordered us to do it this way" then the real issue is the CEO's orders and unless the CEO changes those orders, no effective change will happen. Is it likely that the CEO will change the orders without a compelling argument predicated on a thorough understanding of the orders and their impact? Since we know that it is improbable to effectuate a change in the CEO's orders without the requisite understanding, the real focus should be on understanding the reasoning and then continuing on the 5-Why process with this new information.

Many times a 'why' answer will tread close to ignoring the second key lesson (don't solve the issue with an answer to a why). Going back to the organizational 5-Why example, a reasonable person might conclude, based on the stated answer, that if we somehow achieve cohesion the problem will be solved. But is the only reason that the division loses money a lack of sales and marketing cohesion? Or are there other reasons as well? If we assume that this lack of cohesion is the only reason for the losses, then a single iteration of the 5-Why should suffice to detect and identify the real issue.

However, it is probable that there are other primary and contributing factors as well. By making every effort to avoid answering a why question with a possible implied overall solution, we are likely to get to the most significant factor(s). Once the real issue has been detected and identified, we can repeat the 5-Why process as many times as needed to uncover additional contributing factors and influencers.

Key Takeaways:
1) By channelling our inner toddler and asking 'why' repeatedly, we can discover the root issue behind the problem.
2) 5-Why is a recognizable process for this discovery.

CHANGISTICS TAKEAWAY #5: SUCCESSFUL 5-WHY RELIES ON EMOTION EXCLUSION.

The final impediment to a successful 5-Why process is the injection of emotion as part of the 'why' answering. This impediment is perhaps the most pervasive and common. After all, we are humans with real emotions and what we see, encounter, experience and act on are influenced by our emotions. This is especially true when things aren't going quite right or worse, are outright failing. We have invested part of ourselves, our time, our emotion, and our resources to be part of a success story. If it turns sour, so does our disposition. We don't want our personal investments to be for naught and if, after effort, the tide still hasn't turned, we are understandably not happy about it.

Unfortunately, if we let these emotions creep into our why answers, we will actually travel further from the real issue. It is too easy to blame someone or something for all of the troubles. But if this emotion is part of our answer then the why train will go down the wrong track. We will spend unnecessary time and resources digging deeper into why the person we blame is at fault rather than discovering what process or circumstance drives the issue. If ever there was a time for "just the facts, ma'am" this is it.

Now that the real problem has been identified, it is worth discovering what is causing this problem. One way of discovering the causes is through use of the Ishikawa (or fish-bone) diagram.

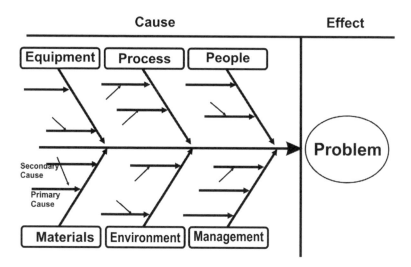

Developed by Karou Ishikawa in the 1960s, this method is frequently used to diagnose problems in the manufacturing environment. It is a critical tool in quality management and is transferable to virtually any problem in any environment. While the prototypical diagram uses the 5-Ms + 1 (man, machine, method, material, measurement, environment) we can also customize for any other environment.

Let's reconsider our weight loss scenario with its assumed real issue of lack of self-worth and self-confidence. We will first need to create categories of causes and potential causes. For simplicity's sake, let's split people into family and non-family. We can also create past events and current events categories. Perhaps we would also add finances and environment to round off our customized cause categories. If we use a hybrid of 5-Why and fishbone, our template might now look like this.

But if this emotion is part of our answer then the why train will go down the wrong track.

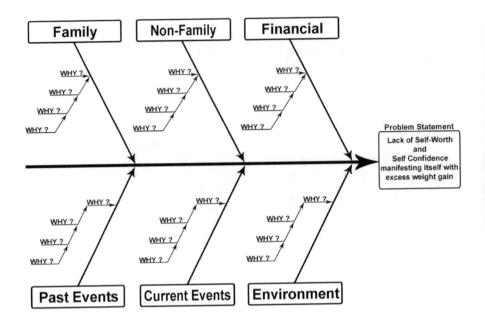

The problem statement is actually a hypothesis or a starting place. We start with what we consider a possible cause and work backwards through the cause categories and their respective why answers. This exercise is especially powerful if we remain flexible to change the problem statement as more causes and answers are discovered.

Alternatively, we could start with the cause categories and their respective why answers and either confirm or alter the ensuing problem statement. By staying flexible, we may even discover additional cause categories or cause categories that are as impactful on the problem statement as the original categories. Either way, we will have travelled significantly closer to the real issue and its underlying causes.

For example, let's say we explore past events as a potential cause of our low self-esteem. First, we'll ask why are past events relevant. Perhaps we'll answer by describing a time we were picked on by so-called friends in second grade. We might follow up with a "why would that impact our self esteem?" Perhaps we'll then answer with an "it encouraged others to pick on me?" We can ask why a few more times and get a "people who didn't even know me started picking on me" and "even teachers started picking on me".

PLAN

By going through the 5-Why for each cause and potential cause, we are striving to understand not only what has affected us but why it has impacted us. And once we better understand all of the whys, we will unearth the root cause(s). Once we have the root cause, we can address the real issues and move forward.

Key Takeaways:
1) *When confronted with problems or issues, we as humans have difficulty separating our emotions from our intellect.*
2) *Using Ishikawa's Fish Bone and 5-Why we can discover root causes without being clouded by our emotional responses.*

CHANGISTICS TAKEAWAY #6: DIVORCING FROM EMOTION IS CRITICAL TO SUCCESSFUL CHANGE.

I was recently leading a session on better change management at a logistics industry forum when I polled the audience to discover who was divorced or was going through a divorce. There were a few hands raised. I chose one woman who had her hand raised and inquired as to whether it was current or past and how well it proceeded. After an initially awkward moment, her answer of "not well" was not terribly surprising. While I didn't inquire as to the nature of the "not well", my point was to highlight a personal change where separating fact from emotion is quite difficult if not almost impossible.

Divorce is perhaps one of the most tumultuous combinations of change and emotion. If there is an additional child custody component, the potential for volatility increases exponentially. Having experienced both these life-changing ordeals myself, I can certainly speak with some authority regarding the changes and how best to react. Let's just say that my reactions going through the ordeal were both expected, and at the same time, counterproductive to my goals. In other words, I once again learned lessons from the school of hard knocks.

Without rehashing all the sorry details, suffice to say all the proceedings were heavily influenced by raw emotion. And as is the case in these types of cases, each action or reaction set in motion a cascading waterfall of emotional responses which ultimately clouded my ability to perceive reality or act rationally.

In retrospect, I let emotions rule the day. Would the outcome have been any different had I made a concerted attempt to distance myself from my emotions? While I will never definitively know, I would certainly have been more level-headed throughout the ordeal and might have conserved resources by not reacting emotionally and through a better understanding of the process and its players. I might not have affected the change, but I certainly could have reacted better to it.

Many a songwriter has written about having to go through hell to get to heaven. Certainly, there is no doubt that we have the ability to grow stronger from adversity and can learn many important life-long lessons from the school of hard knocks. But why should we have to make it harder on ourselves? Aren't some of life's lessons tough enough, without us adding fuel to the flames?

There is nothing wrong with feeling emotion and with having emotional reactions to some of life's changes. After all, we are human and our complex emotions are what separate us from other species. But once it comes down to making a change or moving forward after an involuntary change, we need to focus our efforts on the task at hand. By leaving emotions (as far as possible) at the door, we will be better able to confront reality and deal with it in a constructive fashion. We will better be able to discover the real issues and not be distracted by emotional diversions.

One point of distinction is that while we are attempting to discover and detect an issue, we should attempt to keep our emotions in check so we don't cloud it; however, when we are trying to come up with creative ways of addressing the identified issue, emotions can play a helpful role in generating these ideas.

Key Takeaways:
1) Emotion is a powerful influencer.
2) Rational thought and action/reaction strategies requires us to divorce ourselves from our emotions (as best we can).
3) Emotion, while a likely detriment to rational thought, is useful for creative or innovative thoughts.

ESTIMATE

Once the real issue has been identified, the actual planning can commence. There are three distinct processes that must be followed for successful planning: definition of scope and resources, estimation of potential risk with the detected issue and overall risk-management of real and potential risks.

While we have seemingly identified the real issue through objective investigation and discovery methods (5-Why, and so on), it's not enough to go charging ahead with a solution. Assuming that our discovery has identified the real issue, we must now define the scope of both the problem and its intended solution(s). Defining the scope of the problem is another way of estimating the impact of the detected change. And perhaps the best way to estimate the likely impact of change is to capture critical information using a project charter tool.

Changistics as a process for successful change uses different tools, such as project charters, Intelligent Fast Failure, 5-Why and so on. While not every change initiative will require all of the tools or be used to their maximum potential, every successful change will borrow from the toolbox. In this regard, a project charter is a basic tool that can have its complexity and content modified for the particular application.

Assuming that our discovery has identified the real issue, we must now define the scope of both the problem and its intended solution(s).

PROJECT CHARTERS

This tool is incredibly useful not only in the corporate world, but in our personal lives as well. There is incredible benefit to both the requisite thought process and the process of writing it down. Both help to focus our attention where it matters most; on the matter at hand. While organizational project charters can be quite formal and daunting, both in their format and content, personal project charters don't require the same pomp and circumstance. What's important is that the key questions, resources and support are identified and recorded. This is the epitome of expectation management. Without it, the project runs the risk of floundering or of over-extending beyond the available resource capabilities.

The project charter captures the 'what, why, when, where, who' and even a generalized 'how' of any project, including our change initiative.

What: What is this project all about? What does it hope to achieve? The answers to these two questions not only comprise the estimate step, but also the choose (the desired outcome) step as well.

Why: Why is this project necessary (for example, financial reasons or other impact on the status quo)? This might also address, why the project is necessary now.

When: Assuming we get approval for the project, when will we start and end this project (approximate timeline, including relevant milestones)?

Where: Where will this change be effected (locally, regionally, nationally, or globally)?

What x2: What resources will we need? What will this cost (financial)? What return will this generate? What risks are we planning for? What other risks might be present?

Who: Who is the sponsor of this change initiative? Who will be on the project team? Which executives and managers will need to lend their team members to assist with the project? Who will be affected directly and indirectly?

How: How do we expect to achieve a successful and enduring result? What methods will we use? How do we expect to employ appropriate risk management?

All of these issuess must be addressed, with appropriate levels of detail, in the project charter. Naturally, this is almost a project in itself and will require significant time, research and effort to achieve success. But is all of this really necessary simply to define the opportunity?

Let's consider an alternative scenario. We have participated in the 5-Why process and believe that we have identified the real issue. Assume that this identification is accurate and we start devising a solution for the problem without a project charter. Let's further assume that senior management has given us approval to devise and implement the solution.

Do we know their expectations, other than "solve the problem"? How will we manage these informal expectations, especially once significant resources are requested? How prepared are we for the inevitable 'bumps in the road'? How prepared are the sponsors for these same bumps in the road? How will we handle the inevitable request to extend the solution reach to address a problem not now identified or planned for?

On a simple basis, the project charter formally captures project expectations so that there are no expectation surprises. Everyone knows what is expected, what resources will need to be employed, who will be involved and in what timeframe. While a project charter by itself doesn't guarantee project success, it does provide a tangible roadmap for the project path. Furthermore, bumps in the road are treated as such, addressed and mitigated so the project path can continue forward.

Most importantly, the project charter effectively combats scope-creep. Without the scope being clearly defined in the charter, it is inevitable that new goals will creep into the original plan. It may be that original intended goal was to solve a manufacturing issue with Machine X in Indiana, but now it's covering Machine X across the country. We may then ask, why wouldn't we want to extend the solution to all of the other similar machines, especially since our processes are uniform everywhere?

Without the scope clearly defined, we would take our surface observation and run with it, ignoring the additional resources necessary and the individual location idiosyncrasies inherent with each location (staff and so on.). Is there budgetary flexibility to account for the additional resources necessary or will we be forced to make it happen with only the original resources? Are there environmental idiosyncrasies (such as different humidity, ambient temperatures and so on) that might impact the machinery's operation and productivity?

Without clear scope definition, we also open ourselves to the accelerated impact of project failure. With every project, there is a potential risk of failure. This risk factor exponentially increases with exposure. If the project fails with clear scope definition, only Machine X in Indiana will be affected. If scope creep is allowed, than every Machine X across the country will be adversely affected by the change failure. What is the financial impact of this additional risk exposure?

If the failure occurs, the financial impact will not only be measured in the actual dollars spent on the change, but also on the financial impact on customers, who undoubtedly will suffer from the failed change itself and the time spent remedying it. Another impact is the impact on the people involved with the change. If the failure is impactful enough, then 'heads will roll'. An organization might lose key contributors either by dismissal or resignation in the wake of the failure.

Finally, there is goodwill impact. Undoubtedly, information regarding this failure will spread within the organization, within the industry and sometimes even to the general public. This is likely to have an impact on the organization's good name, leadership role within its industry and perhaps its credibility.

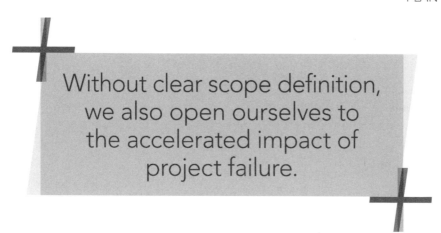

Without clear scope definition, we also open ourselves to the accelerated impact of project failure.

One clarifying note: There is nothing wrong with achieving additional benefits to a change initiative other than the ones realized from meeting of the goal. The problem arises when the goal itself expands beyond what was originally planned, especially if additional unplanned for, and unapproved, resources are necessary to achieve the now-expanded goal.

In a conversation with Garen Smith, board member of Handy & Harman Ltd (a diversified global industrial company), former CEO of Unimast (a wholly owned subsidiary of WHX Corporation) and advisory board member for a large, privately held company, I inquired about his experience with the nature of change management expectations. His response included items that must be included with any project charter, including predicted timescale. In Garen's experience, it takes at least six months of intense work, constant monitoring and communications and socializing within the company to make a shift or change in the business. As the change unfolds, there will be those who are shown either to be unqualified or unwilling and these people need to be either reassigned or removed.

Furthermore, the customer(s) are very important to this process and it's critical that they be fully informed of their value proposition once the change is enacted. It certainly should not be a surprise that Voice of Customer (VOC) is a critical component of most business process management initiatives (TQM, Six Sigma and similar). Finally, key risks must be constantly identified and monitored in an iterative process. For change (or any) project success, time and other expectations must be catalogued and recorded in the project charter. If we can manage expectations from the outset, then there will be a reduced likelihood of adverse surprises later on.

We can further put this into perspective by looking at losing weight, a personal change initiative. More often than not, the excess weight gain is symptomatic of a larger underlying issue (such as lack of self-confidence/self-worth). If we assume that this issue has been identified, the goal would then be to address this issue. While a personal change initiative doesn't necessarily require a formal project charter, it does require realistic planning. Before embarking on this project, several critical sub-issues must be realistically and objectively researched and addressed.

These sub-issues would be likely to include how much time is necessary to successfully mitigate the primary issue, the financial resources needed, other resources that might be required, who will be on the support team and how much support will they realistically give, how setbacks will be handled, and how to know when the goal has been achieved.

If the personal project to mitigate the lack of self-confidence/self-worth is underway, adding the goal of being involved in a fulfilling relationship, would qualify as scope-creep. Now (s)he is simultaneously attempting to mitigate a serious personal issue and at the same time enter into a relationship whose success directly relies on addressing the first goal. It is probable that, in an effort to achieve the second scope-creep goal, the effort on the primary goal will be diminished which will, in a vicious circle, directly impact the probability of relationship success. The result will be failure to achieve either goal at a significant personal cost, including a deepening of the real issue.

Key Takeaways:
1) *Project charters provide the who, what, where, when and hows for any project or change initiative.*
2) *If it's not clearly defined and recorded, the project scope will probably change (scope creep).*
3) *If those involved do not know their specific roles and the specific resources they must deliver, conflict is likely ('he said/she said').*
4) *There is no substitute for absolute trust in successful project completion.*

INTELLIGENT FAST FAILURE

Typically, a failure that occurs in the later stages of the change process will involve significant investments of all types and will have occupied significant time. Essentially, this process could be considered slow, stupid failure. The slow portion is self-apparent by the length of time it has taken for the process and subsequent failure to play out. The stupid portion is due to lack of appropriate planning in the planning phases and not enough consideration and/or experimentation of other alternatives.

Dr Jack V Matson, author of *Innovate or Die* (Paradigm Press, 1996), refers directly to this point, when he talks about the necessity of Intelligent Fast Failure (IFF). While we previously discussed IFF, I had the opportunity to have an extended conversation with Dr Matson during which I inquired about how IFF might work itself into a change process. He elaborated on the three distinct phases of IFF: 'Creative', 'Innovative' and 'Market'.

IFF's 'Creative' phase starts with a multiplicity of ideas. These ideas can be generated using any number of idea-generating methods (such as brainstorming, brain-writing, and so on). During the idea generation exercise, 100 or more ideas might be generated. In the days following, these ideas can be winnowed down to 20 or 30 viable ideas. The other ideas will be eliminated due to their non-viability, non-practicality, or other governing factors that would absolutely preclude their inclusion.

Although the multiplicity of ideas is typically encountered in an organizational environment, it can also be applied to personal change initiatives as well. Since we are all keenly aware of "there's more than one way to skin the cat", we just need to allow ourselves the opportunity to consider as many alternative solutions as possible. We can either explore these alternatives ourselves or with the help of other trusted family, friends and contacts. The important thing is that, at this stage, all ideas are to be recorded, regardless if they seem ridiculous or impossible. At this stage, it's all about idea generation and not actually judging any of them.

Once all of the ideas are in (or after a predetermined period of time has passed), we can winnow down the options. With a personal change, it's likely that we won't start with 100 ideas or end with 20-30, but if we end up with ten possible ways to achieve the goal, then we will have successfully implemented the IFF 'Creative' phase.

For example, let's brainstorm on ways to lose weight.

We could:
1. Starve ourselves for one day a week
2. Eat less junk food
3. Eat no junk food
4. Eat junk food only on weekends
5. Eat junk food only on business trips
6. Join a gym
7. Get a personal trainer
8. Learn to dance
9. Undergo medical bariatric surgery
10. Have liposuction
11. Take diet pills
12. Start a journal to record everything consumed
13. Make public our weight loss goal and incremental progress
14. Go for a walk every day
15. Go for a bicycle ride every day
16. Take up rodeo
17. Go into professional limbo dancing
18. Take up mountain climbing
19. Go to Pamplona, Spain, and run with the bulls
20. Go to marines boot camp
21. Run in circles for half an hour every day
22. Get rid of the office chair and stand instead

23. Have a treadmill underneath the desk and use it
24. Don't use the elevator, even if your office is on the 83rd floor
25. Watch Biggest Loser and subliminally hope the contestants' hard work will inspire our own excess weight to disappear
26. Magic
27. Hypnosis
28. Wish upon a star (makes no difference who you are)
29. And so on…

Many of these ideas are impractical, useless, or even worse, dangerous, but the point is to record all of them without judgment. Once all of the ideas have been recorded, judgment can be applied to them to winnow out those ideas that just won't realistically work. The ten (or so) remaining ideas form the basis of the research step.

At this point, extensive research should be conducted into the remaining ideas. Have these ideas been tried before? Have they failed before? Why did they fail? Have these ideas succeeded before? Why did they succeed? It's also possible that the problem or issue that the ideas are addressing has already been solved by someone else. It is considerably faster and less expensive to modify an existing idea to fit your personal (or organization's) specifics, than it is to 'reinvent the wheel'.

Once the research has been completed, the 20-30 remaining ideas will have been whittled down to three to five good ideas. However, a critical part of the research stage is having the open-mindedness to consider previously unconsidered ideas generated from the research itself. Thus, it is possible that the remaining three to five ideas may include an idea or two that wasn't part of the original 100 ideas. If done expeditiously, the 'Creative' phase might only take several weeks. From here, IFF moves to the 'Innovative' or 'Prototyping' stage.

During the 'Innovative' phase, the full efforts of planning, risk management and experimentation take hold. Essentially, we are able to employ a system of accelerated non-linear experimentation, where we are systematically working on more than one idea at the same time. While the actual prototyping may take longer than the several weeks of the 'Creative' phase, it still allows for a significantly faster discovery of either the one good idea to put into motion, or the need to go back to the drawing board.

When failures subsequently occur during experimentation, they are carefully noted and lessons are learned. These lessons can immediately be employed with all experimented scenarios. It is these failures and the lessons learned that ultimately lead to a better final market-ready product or service.

For our personal changes, trying one or more of the ideas over prescribed durations will result either in incremental progress towards the change or no noticeable difference. The key is to record this information and any other factors that may have been present while doing the experiment. For instance, if you chose to walk every day, but didn't get much sleep during one of the experiment weeks, this lack of sleep factor must be noted and recorded, especially if those results were different and/or unexpected.

Many organizations will float trial balloons towards the end of the experimentation phase to garner and understand end-user (customer) feedback and reaction. At times, this will allow for revisions and modifications to the idea; at other times, it will force a significant overhaul of the idea, or the scrapping of the idea altogether. Either way, the outcome will have been accomplished quicker, and at a lower cost, than a full market introduction without any alternatives.

Once all of the information has been gathered and the last remaining idea has been revised, modified and strengthened, it is ready for the full-scale market introduction. In this 'Market' phase, the idea is being fully disseminated, but the smart organization still has its eyes and ears open for the possibility of unanticipated feedback and/or reactions. If the planning was done with the appropriate risk management, the organization will be able to quickly and appropriately react to the unanticipated and proceed forward unabated.

Key Takeaways:
1) *Intelligent Fast Failure (IFF) is an effective method for rapid limited experimentation.*
2) *IFF provides a means of quick learning from experiments that don't work, resulting in a more successful final product.*
3) *It's better to make quick limited resource experiments than large, slowly moving, heavy resource experiments.*

CHOOSE

Somewhere in all of the ideating and planning, we might have neglected to pay attention to perhaps the most important part of all of this; desired final outcome. Often, this final outcome will be the usual corporate goals; to increase revenues and profits, reduce costs, increase value to stakeholders/shareholders, to be recognized as a solid corporate citizen, to be seen as innovative and progressive, to be added to the list of best companies to work for, and so on. While the particular issue at hand might allow for a final outcome of all of these, it's much more likely that the desired outcome will be significantly more limited and focused. Finding this focused final outcome is essential to shepherding the idea through the 'Change' process successfully.

If we were talking about our flight example, the desired final outcome is limited to a comfortable ride for the duration of the flight. If the desired final outcome had been a speedy journey, we might have chosen to endure a bumpier ride that would end up getting us to our destination faster, over a smoother ride that would delay arrival. Of course, the desired final outcome of any part of a flight is a safe landing, but that should have been an automatic consideration for each and every facet of the flight, so does not merit special mention.

Our industrial example (Machine X) allows us to choose from myriad desired final outcomes. Are we looking for reduced downtime, faster cycle time, higher output, lower material consumption, decreased cost of operation, special operations, reduced setup times, or something else? We need to be focused on a pri-

> Finding this focused final outcome is essential to shepherding the idea through the 'Change' process successfully.

mary final desired outcome and ultimately, identify the course of action based on it. If other ancillary beneficial outcomes emerge, that's all to the good, but they shouldn't be the focus of the 'Change' process. After all, it's impossible to focus finite resources on almost infinite outcomes.

Finally, our personal weight loss example likely has fewer desired final outcomes to choose from. It's likely that the desired final outcome will be from this short list: losing weight, being healthier, looking better, feeling stronger, having more energy, living longer and/or having a healthier lifestyle overall. However, we need to start off with a focus on just one of these outcomes, ideally not one that is too broad. Since the stated problem is being overweight, the desired final outcome would be to lose the excess weight, with some of the other outcomes occurring naturally as a result.

Key Takeaway:
As the Cheshire Cat (in Alice in Wonderland) stated, "If you don't know which way to go, any road will take you there." Where is it that you want to go? What specifically do you hope to achieve? How will you get there? Answering these questions is the key to successfully moving forward.

IDENTIFY

We have detected our issue, estimated its potential risk(s) and chosen our optimal result. Now we need to identify the course of action that will remedy the issue. We have previously discussed the identification of the flight course of action, so we continue with the other examples.

If we were looking at our industrial example (Machine X in Indiana), since we probably already identified the issue prior to the 'Idea' phase, we now have our chosen few ideas from which to select. We need to pick the idea that will best address the issue while also mitigating estimated and unknown risks.

Since randomly choosing isn't optimal, this process is best when incorporating subject matter experts, past experiences, team members' knowledge, senior management preferences, financial considerations, potential upsides and possible downsides. All of this requires considerable research and consideration and is likely to require inputs from significant cross-sections of the organization. In effect, a business case will need to be made advocating, positioning and supporting the optimal choice.

For our personal initiative (weight loss), we also need to choose from our chosen few ideas generated during the 'Idea' phase. And like the industrial example, randomly choosing is unlikely to provide an optimal result. Inputs for consideration will probably be provided by your doctor, nutritionist, trainer, coach, family and friends. Financial and time considerations must also be taken into account for

> We must be willing and able to receive information that not only informs, but might even conflict with, our own established viewpoints. We must be able to give equal consideration to this information in our assessment of options.

each of the potential choices. While a formal business case is likely to be an over-kill for a personal initiative, a written pros and cons list will at least allow for a ready risk-reward analysis. However, unlike our industrial or other organizational examples, the final choice is ultimately ours alone to select.

In either example (and technically, also the flight example), communication is the underlying glue holding the 'Change' process together. We must be openly com-municating with all of the relevant stakeholders prior to making and implement-ing a course of action. Whether it is inquiring of ATC about an altitude that offers a smoother ride, talking to machine operators not only within one's own company but others as well or talking with people knowledgeable about sustained weight loss, the ability to communicate in an honest, timely and relevant matter is criti-cal. Of course, this necessarily means that the communication must be a two-way street. We must be willing and able to receive information that not only informs, but might even conflict with, our own established viewpoints. We must be able to give equal consideration to this information in our assessment of options.

Key Takeaway:
Open communication is critical to identifying the way, means and method forward. Without this openness, we expose ourselves and our projects to a GIGO (garbage in, garbage out) risk with all its consequences.

DO

Finally, it's time for the execution of the plan. Whether we view this from the prism of the final stage of a change management initiative ('Plan', 'Communicate', 'Execute') or we've reached the 'Innovation' phase (from our ICI formula – Ideas + Change = Innovation), we must be able to take the definitive actions we've strategized and planned. I must climb the plane to my requested altitude of 8,000 feet, must implement the operating changes for Machine X and must take the actions determined to help me lose weight.

While we will spend more time with actual plan execution later when discussing both the 'Execute' step and the 'Innovation' phase, suffice to say that no plan comes together without actually taking the requisite actions.

Key Takeaway:
After all the planning, we must still execute what we have planned and evaluate it. Otherwise, all the meticulous planning will have been for naught.

EVALUATE

Now that we have taken our action(s), how well did we do?

Did my climb to 8,000 feet result in a smooth, non-turbulent ride? Did the operating changes to Machine X lead to my desired final result? Have the actions that I've taken to help me lose weight, actually resulted in my losing weight?

Assuming we've put into place the proper evaluation tools to measure and track the progress from before the implemented change (baseline) through the implementation and ending at a designated time post-execution, the answer should be clear.

If we've succeeded in achieving our desired final outcome, then congratulations are in order. In a continuous improvement scheme, the process could potentially start over, with an eye towards driving even better results. But for this particular change, the work is over. At 8,000 feet and experiencing a smooth ride, I can revert back to cruise flight monitoring. With Machine X now producing my desired final outcome, I can move on to other operations or other Machine Xs at different locations. With my weight loss achieved, I can work on tweaking my exercise and dietary regimens to maximize my gains.

However, if we have not reached our desired final outcome, we need to figure out what happened and why. In other words, we need to begin the DECIDE process

However, if we have not reached our desired final outcome, we need to figure out what happened and why.

again. With this new iteration, perhaps other choices will be available either in desired final outcome or methods to achieving our original final outcome.

If 8,000 feet is still turbulent, I can decide that I need to go higher or perhaps that a smooth ride is not possible given current conditions. With this new information, I might decide to grin and bear it, turn around or go in a different direction in an effort to alleviate the problem. If Machine X is still not giving me my desired results, I might choose a different operating change, conduct further research or simply decide that the desired final result is not possible in its current incarnation. If I haven't lost any weight, I might decide that I'm doing the wrong exercises; am on the wrong diet; am working with the wrong trainer; consulting with the wrong doctor/nutritionist; or that it's not possible for me to lose weight through diet and exercise. I might decide that I need more drastic actions (for example, bariatric surgery).

All of these potential actions and conclusions are possible through repeat iteration(s) of the DECIDE model and are critical to the planning stage as a whole. While it is possible to reach the final desired outcome with just a single iteration of DECIDE or a similar model, it is much more likely that multiple iterations will be necessary. Through our understanding and acknowledgment that revisions are likely, we are much more apt to see it through to a successful conclusion.

Key Takeaway:
Critical to any business management process is the ability to evaluate how the process is progressing. This evaluation/assessment must be continuous from the start as it gives us the ability to notice anomalies and take corrective actions.

COMMUNICATE

"What if, and I know this sounds kooky,
we communicated with the employees."

What is the real purpose of communication?

I would stipulate that while it is to convey clear, honest, timely and relevant information, there is a much more important purpose – trust building. Nowhere is this more vital than in a rapidly changing environment, where having the ability to predict and/or react in a positive fashion may hold the key to initiative success.

Trust is the glue in any relationship, personal or professional. Without trust, there is no real relationship. Trust may, or may not, be given or earned easily, but once lost, is almost impossible to regain it fully. Trust is especially important when transitioning through the 'Change' phases. We need to be able to trust our team and sponsor. They need to be able to trust us. This trust is truly a "mean what you say and say what you mean" mentality.

Of course, if the 'Change' team has previously worked together, then undoubtedly, trust has been established and maintained and the team members know what to expect from one another. The team leader knows what to expect from each member of the team and the team members know what to expect from their colleagues and their team leader. It is likely that this trust has been established through words and actions; both forms of communication.

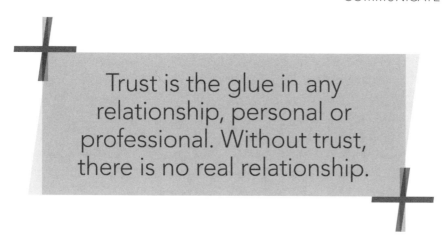

Trust is the glue in any relationship, personal or professional. Without trust, there is no real relationship.

For a team that has not worked together before, there needs to be a leap of faith (or two) for a genuine sense of trust to manifest itself. What are the prospective 'believers' really asked to believe? They are asked to believe that they will earn a PROI for their faith, given trust and, of course, their time, effort and emotion.

So, for a team leader wishing to move forward with new ideas, the first question becomes where to start?

COMMUNICATION STRATEGY

As with any other process or initiative, communication requires a strategy via which to implement its tactics and tools. In a conversation with Lance Fleming, former President and CEO of Crenlo (Dover Corporation), former executive at Rexnord Corporation and now advisory board member to several private companies, the need for a tangible communication strategy is evident. Lance believes, as a result of his experiences, especially at Rexnord, which included multiple leveraged buyouts and executive leadership changes, that companies need to leverage more of a communication-orientated entrepreneurial mindset. "You can never over-communicate strategy (to everyone) and we do this by getting rid of the need-to-know mentality."

Many of his successes evolved out of a strategy that employed:
- Sharing the deployment of the company's overall strategy
- Growth opportunities (whether through product development or mergers and acquisitions)
- Operational improvements, including key metrics of working capital, inventory turns and on-time quality delivery
- High-level corrective action programs
- Innovation initiatives

This information sharing was primarily facilitated in all hands on deck quarterly employee meetings, where strategy was conveyed and questions were welcomed and encouraged. These meetings were held at all locations so the reach would be to everyone, everywhere.

Additionally, Lance reflected on the quarterly meetings: "We also openly shared:
- risks to the business such as unfavorable market conditions that could cause sales levels to go down
- competitive threats from both domestic and foreign competitors from a pricing or innovation perspective
- the expectation of higher levels of performance from our owners,

All communicated to our employees the need for innovation, cost reduction and best in industry delivery and quality. I found that our employees really appreciated the fact that we shared risks and let them know that there could be a reduction in hours or level of workforce coming if sales went down. I have a saying that 'satisfaction is what you get divided by what you expected to get', hence it is critical to manage employee expectations."

Naturally, this encompassing communication was by design and by strategy for the express purpose of influencing people over the long run and providing ample opportunity for individuals to shine. The results: A fair amount of enthusiasm was generated and an overall spirit of engagement pervaded. The bottom line results: A higher than industry average growth rate.

However, a highly effective communication strategy also acknowledges and addresses the unknown, including possible fears and tools to combat it.

Key Takeaways:
1) Good communication doesn't happen by accident. It is, and must be, an integral component of the overall strategy.
2) It must be employed consistently and constantly at all levels of the organization.
3) It also must be accountable and take into consideration possible fears.

IMPACT
ON FEAR

We've previously discussed fear and its outsized influence in our lives. We can all acknowledge that fear is a powerful force and can, at times, be debilitating. However, there are two types of fear: fear of a known entity and fear of an unknown entity. There are very real differences in these types of fear, how they manifest themselves and, of course, our reaction to them.

Fear of a known entity is almost always based on substance and experience. For example, as a pilot, I fear thunderstorms and icing. Both have the capability to bring down my airplane in an uncontrolled fashion and both have unpredictable qualities to them. Contrary to public opinion, it's not the lightning, hail or even wind that make thunderstorms so deadly, rather its turbulence. These aren't merely speed bumps in the sky, but airplane failure-inducing and gravitational-force maximization that can literally rip wings off the plane. Even airliners and planes significantly stronger and faster take extraordinary precautions not to penetrate thunderstorms. Could anyone then argue that the fear is unsubstantiated or unwarranted?

In that regard, icing is also a perilous danger. Despite the advance of technology, we can only take educated guesses as to where icing will occur or how severe it will be. The weather services will issue advisories for large areas where icing is potentially likely to occur, but even with that, there may or may not be icing on your flight path and it may or may not be more severe than predicted. Icing

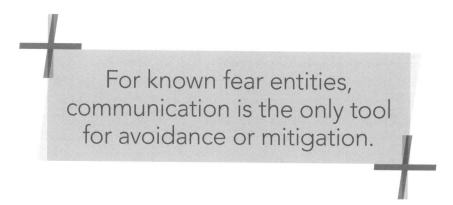

For known fear entities, communication is the only tool for avoidance or mitigation.

has even been known to overwhelm planes with anti-icing systems resulting in deadly accidents. This is also a known entity whose attributes cause rightful fear in a wise pilot and give pause for sober thought.

For these weather aviation hazards, there is no alleviation of the fear itself, rather a prevailing desire for avoidance. Therefore, all my pre-flight planning and en-route planning and monitoring is geared towards avoiding these hazards. ATC, flight services, pilot reports, onboard radar and even in-flight XM weather all provide excellent communication and help in this avoidance. Additionally, every flight has a diversion and alternate routings planned for, just in case the communication is erroneous or inaccurate.

For known fear entities, communication is the only tool for avoidance or mitigation. In the above case, the mitigation might be simply not to take-off in the first place. Would that be inconvenient? Absolutely. Would that be giving in to my fears? You bet. But would I guarantee survival to fly another day? Unequivocally yes. Let's remember that setbacks are ok, if we learn and grow from them.

The other type of fear is more insidious and much harder to define, let alone deal with. This is the very nature of fear of the unknown. We don't even know exactly what to be afraid of, but that doesn't stop us from being very afraid. Where there is fear, there is lack of full effort to the cause. One note: 'fear' is very different than 'concern'. A healthy concern is a positive and useful trait as it allows us to look for potential risks and hazards actively, well ahead of their manifestation. A healthy concern does not prevent us moving forward, albeit cautiously. On the other hand, fear does prevent forward motion. So it behooves us to do everything we can to make the unknown less unknown so it generates as little fear as possible.

We can accomplish this by first getting rid of the 'need to know' syndrome. When leading the team on the change initiative, the team deserves all of the relevant information, in a timely fashion, in a clearly communicated style and with honesty. Simply put, if you have information, the team needs to know. If you don't have the information, they need to know that as well. If the project is facing an adverse challenge or even fighting for its survival, the team needs to know. There must be a commitment to providing this communication. Not only will this build trust and help alleviate fear of the unknown, but it will be a true example of leadership. The fact that all good leaders are also good communicators is no coincidence. Communication and leadership are inextricably tied together as they well should be.

Key Takeaways:
1) Knowledge is power; the power to suppress fear of the unknown.
2) By keeping team/organizational members informed, fear is much less likely to appear.
3) Fear is further reduced by the implicit trust that will flow back and forth, upwards and downwards when everyone is communicating and everyone is informed.

To express this formulaically, we can use the mnemonic CHART:

GOOD COMMUNICATION = CHART = Clear + Honest + Appreciative + Relevant + Timely:

Let's take a closer look at each of these key components.

GOOD COMMUNICATION
= CHART =
Clear + Honest + Appreciative + Relevant + Timely:

CLEAR

Many organizations craft mission, vision and value statements to communicate their goals and expectations internally and externally. Unfortunately, most of these organizations fail the clarity test. Vision statements are notorious for their seeming ability to communicate virtually nothing at all while appearing, on the surface, to communicate something of value. While the language gives the illusion of being aspirational, in reality it exposes a lack of focus and true direction.

For example, consider the following vision statement: "We aspire to empower all our people to achieve their personal goals while delivering the greatest value proposition to our customers." What exactly is this communicating? What exact and/or clear future is their vision communicating?

Let's try this one: "We are committed to providing products and services which meet our customer expectations and our business objectives through a quality system, teamwork and continuous improvement." What are these products and or services? What does a customer or potential customer take away from this?

For an example of a different kind of vision statement, let's look at Microsoft's: "Create experiences that combine the magic of software with power of internet services across a world of devices." As clear as this vision statement is, it's still a departure from its previous vision statement: "A computer on every desktop".

Which of the above examples is clearer? Which one more directly speaks of what the company does and aspires to be?

Of course, the question should be, "why obfuscate and/or hide behind corporate speak, when a clearer option will almost always be better?" The same is true of all of our communications, personal and professional. We can say almost anything in a fashion that not only is clearer but also less verbose, using simpler language and resulting in positive communication and understanding.

One subset of clear communication is appropriate mode. In the conventional logistics world, possible modes could include truck, rail, barge, container, air, and/or some combination. Whatever mode is most appropriate for the commodity, speed and cost would be the one(s) selected and used.

Changistics also relies on selection of the appropriate communications mode. For our purposes, these modes would include face-to-face communication, communication via phone, fax (snail) mail, email and/or video conferencing. Ideally, we would select the mode that is most appropriate for the message, importance of the message and the recipients of the message. The importance of proper mode selection cannot be overstated.

I recall an old United Airlines (cue up the Gershwin) commercial in which the boss of a company was addressing his people regarding being fired by a long-time client. This client no longer felt he was receiving a personal service due to the impersonal types of communication the company was using. The

> Of course, the question should be, "why obfuscate and/or hide behind corporate speak, when a clearer option will almost always be better?"

boss then started handing out airline tickets to his staff members (because, of course, this was an airline commercial) effectively sending everyone out to meet with their clients face-to-face. The commercial ended with the boss flying to see the former long-time client to talk personally with him. The powerful message relayed (besides flying with United) was that there is no substitute for face-to-face communication.

We live in a world in which emails and virtual communications have become the norm, and even preferred, mode of communication. This is necessary in some cases such as where groups of people in different locations need to be addressed. But even then, it should be supplemented with in-person communication. The problem with email is that there is no tone inflection (even if you should type in all caps (DON'T DO IT!), no volume control, no nuance and no body language. If we believe that up to 90% of all communication is non-verbal, are we really communicating effectively via email?

Here's another question: Have you ever misinterpreted an email leading to a miscommunication and perhaps even later an apology? The better question should be "who hasn't?" Without all the non-verbal cues present, it is all too easy to fall into a trap of misunderstanding, sometimes with disastrous results.

The other issue with our over-reliance on email is that we tend to hide behind it, especially in critical conversations (giving bad news). When we do not communicate bad news personally, we are sending the message that the recipients are not even worthy of a personal conversation. What does that do for the recipient's sense of self-worth and motivation? What impact will that have on the rest of the team? If we are managers and leaders then we need to lead, especially when bad news is being conveyed. We owe this professionalism to our team, even if it is personally difficult for us.

Email is appropriate for the short, quick, messages, for yes/no-type answers and for brief fill-in-the-blanks-type questions. For anything that requires more than a line or two, email (as a standalone mode) is not very effective.

While there is no real substitute for face-to-face meetings, video conferencing provides an efficient substitute. Video still loses some of the big-picture non-verbal cues, especially with perspective, but does capture a significant portion of the other non-verbal cues. There should be no opportunity to miss nuance, body language, tone, volume and inflection from a properly setup video conference.

Another subset of clear communication is the words themselves.

However, it is all too easy to rely on technology to conduct a critical conversation. We still run the very real risk of conveying the wrong message when not meeting in person.

To be clear (after all, we are talking about clear communication), I am a big advocate of integration of new technologies to be more efficient and effective, but not as a substitute for being human and being a professional leader. My personal philosophy includes in-person communication wherever and whenever possible.

Another subset of clear communication is the words themselves. We sometimes downplay the importance of this by referring to it as 'simple semantics', but specific words have specific meanings. Even more important is the intent of the words. We sometimes delude ourselves into thinking that intent can be masked by neutral words. But it's just that, a delusion. Somehow the true intent of the communications always comes through (except via email).

When we are working in and/or with teams, word usage and intent take on significant roles. If our intent is to be positive, helpful, appreciative and/or supporting, then our words must reflect our intent. Likewise, if our intent is negative, adversarial, confrontational and/or demeaning, even neutral words won't cover it up.

> We want to be of assistance, but this assistance must be in the realm of facilitating their individual and team goal-orientated efforts. The words we use will either support these causes or unwittingly subvert them.

Of course, we want to get the most from our teams. We want to encourage them to reach out, broaden their horizons, create, innovate and lead sustainable change. We want to be supportive without actually doing their work ourselves. We want to be of assistance, but this assistance must be in the realm of facilitating their individual and team goal-orientated efforts. The words we use will either support these causes or unwittingly subvert them.

There has been much recent discussion about the pros and cons of a decision-orientated atmosphere. When we are prone to making decisions, we effectively cut off the ideation, dynamic debate and the opportunity to consider other options. When we postpone our decision making in lieu of team consensus and the clear outcome of the team's research and other efforts, we have actually considered many more options than we would otherwise have done. And more considered options will ultimately lead to more robust solutions.

The words we use quickly convey to the team whether a decision has been made. If we start a meeting with an opinion relating to a single option, we are essentially asking the team to agree or disagree; we are asking them to vote. Similarly, when we ask or demand someone to defend their position, we are not providing an atmosphere for alternative exploration. There is a time for position language, especially when critically evaluating a pool of options, but not while there are still viable and potential options left to consider.

Key Takeaways:
1) Communication clarity relies on meaning what we say and saying what we mean.
2) So if we mean to nurture an atmosphere and environment in which multiple options can be considered while allowing team member freedom to explore, then our words must reflect it.
3) Employing the appropriate method of communication for the message and audience is of critical importance to how it is received.

HONEST

This trait is not to be confused with overall honesty. While I do believe that honesty is the best policy, I can also make strong arguments for the 'little white lie' when it pertains to many interpersonal communications. How many of us will always answer this classic question from our significant other honestly: "Honey, does this outfit make me look fat?" If the outfit is truly the culprit, perhaps we can answer the question more honestly. But what if the outfit has nothing to do with it? You want to answer honestly but you don't want to hurt the other person's feelings. All I can advise is to tread carefully, my friends. Tread carefully…

What I am really referring to is dishonest communication regarding the status of the project or any of its components. For example, let's say that the project has fallen behind schedule for the next milestone and is in danger of going over budget. You and your team are acutely aware of the status, have been diligently working to correct and catch up, but to no avail. Your sponsor calls you into her office for a status update. What do you tell her?

Often, we will choose words that allow us to position the status in a benign way, if not outright fib a little (or a lot). We might employ an "if you can't beat them, confuse them" mentality. We might even say "we're a little behind, but I'm sure we'll be right back on schedule in no time" or that we're a little over budget, but can recover that in a later stage. Our hope is that we can buy more time to get everything back on track.

Let's say your sponsor takes you at your word (and why not, she trusts you are telling her the truth). She will have no reason to worry or be concerned that there are significant and potentially lethal (to the project) hazards afoot.

But there are no real secrets in an organization, and before long, another senior manager finds out about the issues. If this other senior manager is friendly to your sponsor, she will advise her of her findings and you will be called in again to explain the discrepancy. Unfortunately, you will probably exit the meeting with her having less trust in you or your ability to lead the project successfully. Your stature and influence will be diminished. And you will still be faced with all of the initiative's challenges.

However, let's say the other senior manager is a rival to your sponsor. As rivals are prone to do, he will want to show up your sponsor publicly, demonstrating that she is not in touch with her own projects and people. His aim will be to diminish her stature and influence. At the executive meeting, he will ask her about the project and its status. She will respond with all the optimism that you had built up in her with your less-than-honest report. She will then be confronted, in front of her peers and superiors, with the adverse facts and be asked to reconcile the conflict. What do you think will happen to her, to you and perhaps to the project itself? What if she pulls the plug on the initiative and summarily ends the project in an attempt at damage-control? What will you tell your team?

All this reverts back to the trust issue. The sponsor trusts the team leader not only to lead the initiative forward but to communicate its status honestly, even if it's not good news. The team leader trusts the sponsor to support the project and provide both additional resources and senior management cover when things aren't going quite right. Additionally, the team members trust the team leader to direct the project ably and communicate honestly about the status and other relevant information, while the team leaders trust the team members to complete their tasks responsibly and to communicate relevant issues honestly.

Key Takeaways:
1) *All trust is lost if there is any dishonest communication between any of the parties. It truly is a garbage in/garbage out entity.*
2) *Save the little white lies and misplaced optimism (if applicable) for the non-project-related personal interactions and be honest regarding the project.*

APPRECIATIVE

If the primary purpose of communication is successfully to convey thoughts and information effectively, can we accomplish this if our audience is disengaged and/or dispirited?

Everyone needs to feel acknowledged and for their success to be recognized, even the minor successes. Most people want to feel appreciated for their hard work and efforts, yet many leaders and organizations fail at this basic level. The expectation is that "that was part of your job" or worse, "what do you want, a medal or a monument?" These same organizations may recognize those that "hit it out of the ballpark" using whatever subjective criteria is the flavor du jour. But even a thank you for a great job done or a sincere pat on the back has as much chance of being communicated as I have winning the next Powerball drawing or any other lottery.

Even simple displays of that lack of gratitude and appreciation lead directly to disengagement, dispiritment, disillusionment and resentment. Maybe our team members are already conditioned to not being thanked or appreciated for every good thing they accomplish. Maybe we feel that their success is to be expected, after all, that's why we hired them. Maybe we feel that constant shows of gratitude and appreciation will come across as insincere.

Regardless, when we show sincere appreciation and gratitude, even something as simple as an informal "thanks", we are showing that we care about that person and what he or she accomplished. We are actively engaging with that person and maintaining that level of engagement. On every level, that person recognizes and appreciates this show of appreciation and a positive vicious cycle is created with mutual appreciation being the net result.

Of course, this is relatively easy to manage when the news is all good. It is significantly more difficult when the news is not positive, negative in part, or simply challenging. As managers and team leaders, we tend to be direct and want to address the challenge and/or bad news immediately. Often when there is both good and bad news, the manager will jump straight to the bad news without acknowledging the good news. The result is a dispirited team that will just be going through the motions and not fully engaged with the challenge ahead.

Key Takeaways:
1) If we are to lead our teams and organizations through both the good and the challenging times, we need to accentuate the positive at every opportunity.
2) We need to allow our teams to revel in the glory of their accomplishments even if there are obstacles ahead.
3) We need to maintain our team's full engagement and spirits consistently.
4) And we need team engagement to address, and detour around, any immediate and future barriers.

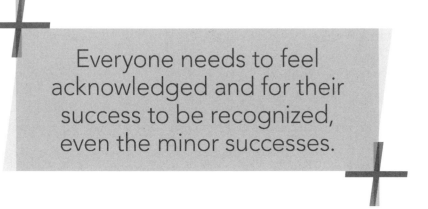
Everyone needs to feel acknowledged and for their success to be recognized, even the minor successes.

RELEVANT

We live in an age of information overload. For those who care to seek it out, we have more information than we could possibly process coherently. A phrase has even been coined, summing up this scenario: paralysis by analysis. So if there was ever a time to communicate only the relevant information, it would be now.

The issue is in determining just what is relevant and to whom is it relevant. The issue increases in complexity with project teams and the communication between team members. Adding to this complexity is the communications from team leaders upwards to sponsors and back downwards to team members.

Since it is quite difficult and time-consuming for team leaders and team members to sort through all of the incoming information and feedback from the project, different model utilizations are required. Aviation provides such a model through flight briefing and Notice to Airmen (NOTAM) systems.

When a pilot is planning a flight, he is required to avail himself of all relevant information about the departure and arrival airport, weather at both airports and en route between them, significant and air hazardous weather alerts (SIG-METS and AIRMETS), Temporary Flight Restrictions (TFR) (if any) and Notices to Airmen (applies to airports, runways, taxiways, airspace, navigation and general). This is quite a bit of information and can be cumbersome to sift

> For those who care to seek it out, we have more information than we could possibly process coherently. A phrase has even been coined, summing up this scenario: paralysis by analysis.

through. Much of the information is not directly relevant to the flight at hand but is included in the briefing anyway.

For those who receive their briefing online through one of the many authorized aviation websites, the information is segregated into each of the categories, allowing a focus on one area at a time. This system also allows the pilot to scan quickly through information that is not directly relevant, focusing his attention on what is actually important. All of the information that is present can be selected by the pilot at his discretion.

Essentially, this is a moving, selectable database of relevant information. There is no need to choose and sort out to whom each piece of information should go; rather each pilot chooses his own information from the master route briefing. The user is the determinant of relevance.

This model can be applied to any project, personal or professional. Through creation of a repository/database of all information/feedback gathered and received, each member of the team can proceed directly to the information that is most relevant while still retaining access to the remainder of the information. Additionally, team meetings allow for sharing of cross-functional information and big-picture information. The role of the team leader is to provide both perspective and support as the project progresses forward.

For a personal project, a database is just as important, but without the same robustness or comprehensiveness. If we consider our weight loss initiative, we can place information and facts received into the database and sort it as a positive, negative or neutral influence on our projected plan. We can track our progress and exceptions on a spreadsheet, giving us an instant view on our progress and setbacks.

For instance, I created a spreadsheet that tracks my starting weight, weight at the end of each week, the difference (in percentage) from week to week and month to month, as well as the overall percentage weight loss since the start of the initiative. I also keep track of exceptions, such as holidays, travel days, number of days worked out with the trainer, and so on. I can later decide if those exceptions are relevant or not, but for now, it's all there for review and consideration.

Key Takeaways:
1) In all cases, relevant communication allows for all information to be communicated so that nothing is missed.
2) In an ideal system, the potential users of the information have the ability to select what's particularly relevant to their efforts without compromising the ability of others to employ that same selection process.

TIMELY

The great Talmudic scholar, Hillel the Elder stated, "If I am not for myself, who will be for me? But if I am only for myself, who am I? If not now, when?"

How many of us, when presented with the opportunity to present a change initiative, get excited and enthused about the prospects only to be thwarted with a "the timing is not right for this" or "we're not ready for this yet" or even "we do need this, just not now"? Is this a setback owing to poor salesmanship or simply a put-off?

While I believe the reason is most likely to be a case of senior management not wanting to take on the requisite pain inherent in a change initiative, there may be some truth behind their timing opposition. We've all repeatedly heard that there's a time and a place for everything and everything in its own time. Certainly, timing is a legitimate factor when pursuing any initiative, change or otherwise.

This is just as true when it relates to communication and information. How often do we receive information, which would have been quite useful if conveyed to us quickly, only communicated to us much later? How often does an urgent matter come to our attention that was known to others in the organization well before it was made known to us? If we had only had that information sooner, we could have addressed it immediately, so that it never rose to the urgent level.

With our previously mentioned repository/database being created, there should be ample opportunity to enter this information and allow it be accessed and shared by the team.

However, what this doesn't entail is the prolific multiplication of meetings. Many managers truly believe in timely and relevant communication, but fail in the execution. Their mentality is that every time there is some information to be shared, a meeting must be scheduled so that it can be communicated to the team. In the process, significant time is wasted and attention is scattered. After all, who wants to sit in yet another meeting to receive information that could easily have been shared in another, more efficient and productive, manner.

An even worse consequence of this multiplication is that while the team may be physically present, mentally, they will have checked out already. At some point, not only will the information from the meeting fail to stick, but when something truly important (and meeting-worthy) arises that does need to be discussed, holding the team's attention will be very difficult, if not impossible. So let's save the meetings for those discussions that truly require the all-hands-on-deck participation and scope.

Key Takeaways:
1) Respect everyone's schedule.
2) Start and end meetings on time.
3) Ensure that everyone knows what they need to know when they need to know it.
4) Don't inflict filler material on team members or extend meetings (for the sake of it); it wastes everyone's valuable time.

INNOVATION

GENESIS OF INNOVATION

We've reached the culmination of our efforts: Innovation.

But from where does innovation come?

Some will advocate that it's the net product of ideation and/or creative effort. Others may argue that it is (or at least, should be) the continuous outflow of a systematic and cultural personal and/or organizational effort. My personal belief rests with a combination of the two. In other words, the ICI formula we discussed previously.

But what if there were an established tool that anyone could use to focus their efforts towards sourcing innovation? While skeptics might scoff at the notion of using such a tool, instead relying on process, procedure and systems, what if there were really such an option?

Those of us schooled and/or exposed to Lean or Six Sigma are intimately familiar with Ishikawa and his cause and effect diagram to expose root problems. Otherwise known as the fishbone diagram, it doesn't require a great deal of knowledge or complex handling to achieve results. We previously examined Ishikawa but in the more traditional role.

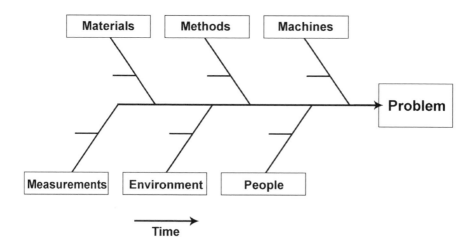

What if we substituted 'problem' for 'focus of innovative effort' or simply 'innovation'? Could such an established and widely-used tool successfully lead to innovation?

I propose that it both could and will, so let's take a closer look.

The beauty and utility of Ishikawa's work is that the headers can be substituted for any other appropriate category and it doesn't necessarily have to follow a particular order. For the sake of this exercise, I'll use the traditional 5M + 1 formula (man, material, machine, measurement, method and environment) to discover potential innovative focus in a typical office setting.

Man

Otherwise known as people, these are the nuts and bolts of any initiative, any operation and any organization. After all, without the right people, there will be no ideation, no changes and no innovation. Thus, exploring "who are the people in your neighborhood" – apologies to Fred Rogers (*Mister Rogers Neighborhood;* PBS: 1968-2000) – is a great place to start.

1. Who is in the office?
2. What is the hierarchical order or reporting order?
3. Are there enough people?
4. Who else should be added?
5. To whom should they report?
6. Are there too many people?
7. Are there other departments with which there will be interaction?
8. Are there external people with whom there will be interaction?

Material

Now that we have looked at 'who', let's continue with 'what'. Exploring the physical things with which we work can also lead to innovative focus. These things can range from supplies to office furniture to raw materials.

1. What supplies do we work with?
2. How effective are they?
3. Should other supplies be added?
4. What, and how much of, those other supplies might be needed?
5. Are there supplies that are not needed?
6. Who provides these supplies?
7. Are they effectively and efficiently supplied?

Machine

An extension of 'what' is automation, or other electronic assistants we use to help us do our jobs. This includes not only our computers, but also the hardware, software, cloud computing, websites, and other related tools.

1. What computers do we use?
2. What peripheral equipment do we use?
3. What equipment do we need that we don't currently have?
4. What equipment do we want that we don't currently have?
5. What software do we/could we/should we use?

6. Is there an app for that?
7. What technologies do we/could we/should we use?
8. Why don't we have equipment we need and want?

Measurement

Now let's look at 'when'. These next explorations get to the heart of how we know what we know. Without diminishing the importance of intuition or gut feeling, ultimately, objective facts are necessary to ascertain the situation fully.

1. How is our performance measured?
2. How is our productivity measured? Our efficiency?
3. Who measures it?
4. Why is it measured?
5. Are there other things we could and should measure?
6. How often is it measured? Why?
7. What is the result of these measurements?

Methods

This next exploration also includes policies and procedures. In essence, we are now answering (or should be answering) the 'why' and 'how'. If we can understand why and how we do what we do, we are much more likely to conjure up new ways in which to improve and build upon it.

1. Do we have a standard operating procedure (SOP) for how we do things?
2. Do we have any other established procedures for how we do things?
3. If we could create or amend any procedure, what would that be?
4. What would a flow chart of each of our activity areas look like?
5. What policies do we have that govern our activities?
6. Do we need to improve? Where? How?
7. Who do we need to influence to make these changes?

Environment

Since nothing exists in a vacuum, an understanding of 'where' we work. both on a macro and micro level, can certainly unlock innovative focus.

We once again reference the conversation with John Surma, who strongly advocates the outsized importance of environment. John references two examples of environment conducive to rapid innovation.

Since nothing exists in a vacuum, an understanding of 'where' we work. both on a macro and micro level, can certainly unlock innovative focus.

John first discusses the emergence of the Shale Revolution, and specifically the emergence of the Marcellus Shale as a source for oil and natural gas. Drilling for oil used to be a cumbersome and expensive endeavor highly susceptible to overall oil and general market fluctuation. Through the emergence of horizontal drilling and fracking – essentially the perfect combination of people, knowledge and capital, US Steel (and others) were able to innovate rapidly and bring to the forefront new technologies to serve the fracking industry. Furthermore, while oil is present in other rock formations worldwide, only the US (and Canada) possess the open access pipeline system, private ownership of mineral rights and deep capital markets to capitalize, truly and successfully, on this revolutionary method of oil and gas drilling.

As another example of environment in action, John talked about his experience in the early 1990s as a partner at Price Waterhouse. In those early days of computer technology, the company had established a think tank in California to explore new technologies. During this time, a new electronic method of auditing was developed (Teammate). One of John's client's heard about this technology, asked for a site visit and was so impressed, that they asked to be a beta tester. Despite the reluctance of others in the firm, John facilitated the testing and the technology became a foundation piece for the systems used today. In fact, during the late 2000s, while John sat on the board of the Bank of New York – Mellon, the bank was considering purchasing a new system, a successor to the original Teammate technology. This further reinforces the notion that once the environment is set for innovation, there is no directional limit to where it can end up.

Here are questions to consider when establishing an innovation environment and/or culture:

1. What does our organizational culture look like?
2. What does our departmental culture look like?
3. What does our physical environment look like?
4. Does this make us happy, unhappy, inspired or uninspired? Why?
5. What could be done to improve the physical environment?
6. What could be done to improve the cultural environment?
7. What could we hope to achieve with changes to the environment?
8. Who do we need to influence to make these changes?

Of course, this list isn't exhaustive, but it is designed to illustrate the power of Ishikawa to focus innovative thought and ultimately lead to useful and practical innovation.

Key Takeaways:

1) A culture of innovation does not require using an already employed innovation mode. Hybrids or even brand new models can and do work.

2) Other business process management tools can be adapted to allow for greater innovation (for example, Ishikawa).

3) Don't look past other business or social models to provide ideas and inspiration for building your organization's culture of innovation.

4) Always be questioning and discovering.

INNOVATION CULTURE DEVELOPMENT

If an organization wishes to inspire and sustain innovation, a culture of innovation is required. And while there are many variations and hybrids within innovation cultures, the basic components remain constant. Of course, this does not mean that innovation cannot survive in a non-innovation culture; it just faces much longer survival odds and its success is likely to be despite the organization's culture and not because of it.

1. Bring in the right people
It all starts with having the right people. A culture of innovation relies on identifying those already present who are inclined towards innovation as well as taking on new people who are, or are predicted to be, innovatively inclined.

No matter how fantastic, cohesive and/or realistic an innovation strategy is, it will be to no avail if the right people aren't behind it.

Quick question: Is your organization identifying, and recruiting, those who are inclined to be innovative? If it is, how do you know that these folks are truly innovatively inclined? If not, what can your organization do to remedy this situation?

2. Develop support at the highest levels
While there have been examples of innovation despite lack of senior management support, they are more the exception than the rule. No matter which

innovation model is employed, a culture of innovation cannot be created, much less sustained, without the continuing support of at least one senior executive.

Does your organization's senior leadership acknowledge, appreciate and take tangible steps to foster innovation? If yes, are they limited to functional business units or are they dedicated resources towards innovation? If no, why are they not taking these steps and how best can we influence a change?

3. Organizational innovation model choices

Even though there has been much written and spoken about, and expounded upon, regarding innovation, there are only four basic models, with almost endless hybrids and variations within them. These models, in ascending order, according to quantities of organizational support/resources, are:

a. Ad-hoc
- Innovation success resulting despite the organizational culture
- No designated organizational ownership
- No dedicated resources
- Network-driven concept selection

b. Dedicated
- Senior executive-driven
- Limited resources allocated
- No official organizational ownership
- Designated criteria for prospective projects
- Specific to functional business unit(s)
- Innovations tend to be adaptive and closely related to core

c. Focused
- Official and formal organizational ownership
- Higher level of resources allocated – still limited in nature
- Greater freedom with criteria – higher levels of transparency
- Multiple functional business units(s)
- Innovations can be transformational but only within the existing organization

d. All-in
- Formal and separate innovation units
- Significant and independent funding

- Greatest freedom with criteria – highest levels of transparency
- Innovation resources are separate from other existing business units
- Innovations are frequently transformational and leading to new businesses separate from the existing core business

For the sake of sustainable innovation and the development of an innovative culture, the last three models are the only ones that should be considered.

What model most closely represents the reality at your organization? How well is this working? What can be improved? What do the resulting innovations look like – are they adaptive or radical/transformational? Are they limited to specific business units or are they entity-wide?

4. Allocation of resources

When all is said and done, the type and level of resources allocated is what truly determines the robustness and sustainability of an organizational culture of innovation. These resources are not only monetary, but include executive time, participating team members and physical resources (such as meeting rooms, IT, and so on).

Even if senior leaders ostensibly support innovation, how active are they in the process? What other managers, team members, funding, time and/or physical resources are designated for these initiatives?

Are ongoing allocations of these resources inextricably tied to tangible success of all the initiatives? If they are, what is the result of initiative failure on the overall culture and continued resource allocation? If not, how does the organization respond to initiative failure(s)?

5. Release the endorphins redux

We've previously discussed the role that humor and even improvised comedy can play in fostering and maintaining a culture of creativity and change, but can it play a crucial role in innovation?

In a study by Aseem Inam at Massachusetts Institute of Technology (MIT), published in the *Journal for Education in the Built Environment*, the answer is an unequivocal yes. Some of the commonalities between comedy and innovation are listed over the page:

No matter how fantastic, cohesive and/or realistic an innovation strategy is, it will be to no avail if the right people aren't behind it.

> By learning from an 'improvised comedy' model, an organization can successfully build upon earlier innovative successes.

- The counterintuitive nature of innovation occurring in an apparently inefficient manner of brainstorming and exploration of all ideas, regardless of viability
- Innovation occurs from a team model where each team member individually contributes through "listening, suggesting, augmenting and extrapolating ideas of their own and of others"
- A critical component is the ability to listen and being sensitive to ambient clues that may or may not be disguised in otherwise mundane environments (for example, bricks, water, and so on)
- Through the suppression of the urge to self-edit and/or judging other, creativity can occur
- Ideas can be more creative when team members are supportive and can add upon, and extend from, the original idea
- Innovation occurs when performers and designers have the courage to take thoughtful risks and to learn from failure by finding a level of comfort with it

Key Takeaways:

1) *To build a winning culture of innovation, we must identify, recruit and retain the right people.*
2) *We need to have support from the highest levels of the organization.*
3) *We must employ an innovation model that has this highest level of support.*
4) *Resources must be allocated in a fashion that will encourage and not restrict innovation.*
5) *By learning from an 'improvised comedy' model, an organization can successfully build upon earlier innovative successes.*

EXECUTE/DO

"It's always good to experience 'cutting edge' technology."

In a discussion with Murray Crane, CEO of Dektrix (an innovative flatdeck intermodal logistics provider) and founder of Raildecks Intermodal, Murray offers a critical checklist for pursuing innovations.

First, is the innovation a trend or a fad? The answer to that question can only be understood via thorough marketing research. Trends are much more likely to be sustainable both in terms of innovation and financing. Even if it is trend-orientated, how long will it take to realize a tangible ROI? Murray further posits: "Without the right fit, there is no sense in going down the road". As an example, he references the early and rapid adoption of Enterprise Resource Planning Systems (ERP). The stated goal was that, through its adoption, efficiencies would be realized and improved upon. For many companies, the adoption revealed an over-reliance on technology without full understanding of the resulting impact on the users and other people. For these companies, there were many unanticipated surprises including module delays and overrun costs, aside from the resulting change-resistance from employees. ERP systems can be wonderful tools but how they fit within an organization, and anticipating potential issues, becomes critical to their ultimate success.

As a corollary, Murray also spoke of recognizing when something in the plan just isn't working. "Ultimately, everything becomes your fault, so you must plan well for every foreseeable event. You must plan for failures... they will inevitably happen. So if something isn't going right, stop and fix it before continuing on."

Next, through planning, forecasting and financial analysis, are you able to bring your innovative vision together with a business plan to ascertain viability? After all, a true test of innovative leadership is believing and staying with the vision of innovative intent. Without it, bringing others on board will be very difficult (if not impossible). This is the critical difference between dreams and visions. The ultimate goal: The innovation must be built on getting revenue and being self-sustainable.

However, ideation and change management are not static linear pieces to this puzzle. They are iterative and recurring.

Thus, we have reached the culmination of both the ideation and change phases; it is now time to execute the plan. However, ideation and change management are not static linear pieces to this puzzle. They are iterative and recurring. The best plans are ones that allow for new ideas, tweaks, modifications and even significant changes, to be ultimately successful. Ideation and change management are not, and cannot, be "set it and forget it" entities. It is in this regard that the 'Innovation' portion of our ICI formula (idea + change = innovation) also incorporates the 'Execute' (plan, communicate, execute) and 'Do' (DECIDE = detect, estimate, choose, identify, do, evaluate).

We previously defined 'Innovation' as a sustainable new entity, process or method. It is not enough simply to create something new and hope for the best. History is littered with examples of innovators (conventional definition) who created and/or invented a revolutionary new product never to realize the benefits themselves.

A perfect example is with a new car in its first model year. Despite all the rigorous planning and modelling, it takes a year or two of it actually being driven for all of the bugs to be identified and designed out. It may indeed be a great car with fantastic features, but it's rarely nominated (in its first year or two) for quality awards or a 'best buy' from the independent reviewers.

This understanding is also why many organizations and their leaders shy away from bleeding-edge technology. They don't want to be the first to try something new, preferring instead to let someone else be the proverbial guinea pig. From the trials and tribulations of the first adopters, a better and more sustainable entity will arise and then, perhaps the organizations standing by will adopt the technology.

Of course, this is really just a modern version of the chicken and the egg, with someone needing to be that guinea pig before others can jump on board and adopt. In this vein, we can use another example from the intersection of sustainability (green technologies), conventional logistics and steel company operations.

The transporting of steel across land is frequently accomplished through the use of flatbed trucks and/or the rail network. Steel, by its very properties, is heavy and requires heavy duty trucking to transport. These flatbed trucks have poor fuel efficiency, and if fortunate, will only average seven to eight miles per gallon of diesel fuel. Diesel is the by-product of the oil refining stage and tends to leave dirty emissions. Even with newly enacted regulations to reduce these emissions, quite a bit still makes it into the air. Diesel is also relatively expensive with the US national average ranging from $2.75-$3.00 per gallon.

There has been a push over the past five years for trucks to use natural gas as an alternative fuel. This natural gas can be either compressed natural gas (CNG) or liquefied natural gas (LNG). CNG has seen the most activity both in engine conversions and infrastructure (specifically, conveniently located filling stations). CNG is approximately half the price of diesel after equalizing units of each and many fleets have started to adopt this technology, even though the engines are 30% more expensive than conventional diesel engines. Overall, the engines pay for themselves, pending mileage driven and are better for the environment. However, there are currently no heavy-duty CNG engines in operation. So if you have a heavy-duty operation, like steel, either underpowered engines have to be used or LNG must be utilized.

LNG is more expensive than CNG but not nearly as expensive as diesel. These engines are also 30% more expensive than diesel engines, but even though heavy-duty engines are in place, there is virtually no supporting infrastructure. Also, with either engine, massive improvements must be made to the supporting maintenance operations.

For these reasons, there are virtually no heavy-duty fleets using natural gas technologies. I have spoken with senior executive leadership at a few of these steel companies and there is a sincere and earnest desire to be on the leading edge of this technology for this type of use. There is even some desire to be innovators, with conversion equipment perhaps being created and used to allow for better rationalized heavy-duty use. But either way, it's only currently at bleeding-edge status with its future sustainability in serious doubt. Will the companies in question be willing to make a significant investment in unproven technology with uncertain results? Or will they stand by and allow someone else to try, learn lessons from and then consider adopting?

Undoubtedly, there is a tangible innovator's risk. Unfortunately, this risk is realized when execution is not complemented with continued ideation, experimentation and change-management strategies. Often, the innovation itself doesn't solve a tangible issue; isn't a product/service that is currently needed or wanted; hasn't been thoroughly debugged; or simply fails to attract any attention. Is this, then, an innovation or execution failure?

While it would be easy for us to chalk it up as another failed invention, gone up in flames or just crazy, in reality, this would be a planning failure. Somewhere in the planning phase, someone didn't ask either the right questions or enough questions. For instance, revisiting the 5-Why process with our new invention might illuminate where the train left the tracks:

This is a brand new innovative mousetrap. (Every year, there are thousands of patent applications for new and improved mousetraps.)

Q1:   Why do we need a new mousetrap? (Or what's wrong with what we currently have in place?)

A1:   The old mousetraps are clumsy, heavy and out-dated.

Q2:   Why (or how) would this solve those problems?

A2:   This is simple to use, light and eliminates the resulting mess.

Q3:   Why would anyone want to switch from the mousetraps with which they are familiar?

A3:   Because it is only logical that if it's easier, lighter and cleaner, people will want it.

Q4:   How do you know that this is what people want?

A4:   Because I would want that from a product improvement.

Where are the problems with this 5-Why example?

If you put on your marketing hat, the problems with this business rationale are glaring. First, the innovator has assumed that logic plays a significant role in buying decisions. Second, the innovator has assumed that people are looking for these particular improvements in a mousetrap. Third, the innovator has assumed that his decision-making processes are the same as the general public's processes. Fourth, the innovator relies heavily on assumptions without any objective backup.

Key Takeaways:
1) *Sustainable innovation requires an understanding of the marketplace and what people within it are likely to want to buy.*
2) *Sustainable innovation requires the ability to make corrections mid-stream.*
3) *Ultimately, an understanding that the innovator's logic and decision-making process might not match precisely with that of the marketplace, is critical to being able to make corrections and revisions.*

EVOLUTIONARY OR REVOLUTIONARY?

"My approach tends to be revolutionary."

Many an innovator and innovation has met with minimal sustainable success primarily due to the 'field of dreams' mentality: If we build it, they will come (Universal Pictures, 1989). Essentially, they have substituted this idea for the rigorous planning and requisite change-management phases. And many times, they will build it and no one will come. Or worse, someone else will come, make some improvements, follow the planning and change stages, acquire objective consumer data and then put out a product that people truly do want and will purchase.

At the surface, there is nothing wrong with the Star Trek mentality either – "to boldly go where no man has gone before". However, this needs to be tempered with the realistic expectation that your journey might, for at least a little while, be a solo one. Essentially, the bleeding-edge issues are one and the same as those of the radical-change instigator.

I've written and spoken extensively about how both radical and adaptive change is necessary for true innovation. The key component to either is degree. Even the best 'out there' idea must be considered under the prism of readiness. Consider the smartphone. The technology had been in place for more than 15 years but we weren't quite ready for it yet (remember the Palm Pilot?). We needed to be brought along slowly. First, the personal digital assistants (Palm in 1996), then email pagers (Blackberry, 1999), then the first iPhone (2007) followed shortly after with Android smartphone (2008). Chances are quite high that if you had invented the Android in 1996 or even 2000, it wouldn't have sold very well. We could have built the best smartphone possible and buyers still wouldn't have come. We just weren't ready for it at that point in time.

This is the premise of radical change through adaptive change. If we looked at the world pre-1995 and then at our current world, we would look upon the smartphone as game-changing, 'reinventing the wheel' technology. But if we looked at the changes incrementally, then each change would be more of a tweak of added functionality and design, rather than a revolutionary approach.

It is through this perspective that we need to evaluate our innovation. Is it evolutionary or revolutionary? Most of us are not ready for a revolutionary approach to anything. It is just too much change, that takes us too far out of our comfort zones, that assumes way too much risk and leaves us too open for criticism or adverse reaction. Most of us are not ready for bleeding-edge. After all, bleeding conjures up images of injury, pain and messiness. Who really wants that?

However, many of us are willing to be evolutionary and try that next great thing (at least to some degree). Depending on the product/service and its features and functionality, we might be willing to take on some change, put ourselves out there (at least a little bit) and assume some risk; all without inviting criticism or

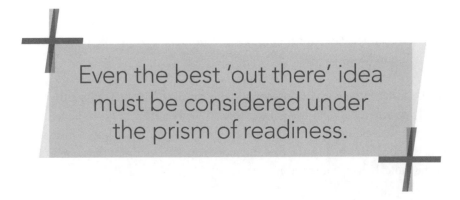

> Even the best 'out there' idea must be considered under the prism of readiness.

adverse reaction. We are more willing to be leading edge. Leading edge has the connotations of being cool, hip, advanced, and visionary. We are considered to be in tune with the rapid pace of today's ever-changing world.

Key Takeaways:
1) *Evolutionary or adaptive change will fit many organization's innovation models.*
2) *There is a difference between leading edge and bleeding edge. Is your market prepared for either?*
3) *Understanding the difference between fads and trends can help an organization weather a fickle marketplace.*

AVIATE, NAVIGATE, COMMUNICATE

With all of the planning, changing and executing, we sometimes have a tendency to overreact to occurrences that deviate from the expected. And let's be clear, there will be deviations or speed bumps along our path to true innovation. If the overreaction is pronounced enough, we can end up dooming our own initiative through our very efforts to correct the deviation. While we could then chalk this up to planning failure (due to our not planning for the deviation or a process for evaluating/correcting), wouldn't we benefit more from not experiencing the failure in the first place, or in this case, not overreacting?

We previously discussed the two natural reactions to change (or in this case initiative deviation): denial and overreaction. Certainly, we cannot just ignore the deviation or pretend that it doesn't exist, but equally, we should not take automatic drastic action at the first hint that something is wrong. It's all about evaluation and a balanced response.

Let's first clarify degree of deviation. If deviation is within the pre-determined acceptable range, we might not have to react or take action at all. After all, this was planned. We might want to investigate, in an effort to reduce future variability, but if we do absolutely nothing, the deviation is still tolerable, the flight is still operating safely and all is in order.

This type of deviation could be seen in aviation, particularly in a plane that doesn't have altitude hold (auto-pilot). We could have the plane trimmed perfectly at our desired altitude and then encounter a gust of wind or minor turbulence that bumps us up. In an attempt to reduce the altitude gain, we might push the nose down slightly. The result would be oscillation that results in minor altitude fluctuations that eventually settle. During this oscillation, we would still be within acceptable altitude range and wouldn't need to take any further action as the plane would settle at our desired altitude. Of course, we would be diligently monitoring our instruments to ensure that the plane was operating as desired.

By contrast, the deviation that demands action is usually of a degree that screams for remedial action.

In aviation, when things go really wrong, such as an engine out or systems failure, the overriding strategy is 'aviate, navigate, communicate', in that exact order. First things first, fly the plane. We must maintain control over the situation and keep the plane flying upright. It is much too easy to lose focus, panic and/or overreact to the situation. Any or all three of these reactions can easily lead to a loss of control and a serious accident. Typically, the actions needed to stabilize the plane are not drastic, but they do require quick action. If the plane can be stabilized, there is a potential opportunity to remedy the situation.

Only once the plane has been stabilized with the pilot firmly in control, does navigation occur. Where are we going now? Where should we be going now? Sometimes, the best possible place to go is behind us or in another unplanned direction. Sometimes the best place to go is an off-airport landing area. When things go wrong, our primary goal is our safety and the safety of our passengers.

With a direction and an idea of where we are heading, we can now communicate with air traffic control (ATC) or others about our emergency. While communication is important, it is easily trumped by the other two actions. This is especially true, considering that all the communication in the world will not, in itself, land the plane safely or resolve the emergency.

Our success in reaching the innovation stage and then being able to capitalize on it depends on our ability to react appropriately to the inevitable deviations from our planning. We must place ourselves in the best possible position to evaluate the situation and then react appropriately and proportionately. We must fly our planes, and when things (or plans) go awry, we must continue to fly in a stabi-

> In aviation, when things go really wrong, such as an engine out or systems failure, the overriding strategy is 'aviate, navigate, communicate', in that exact order. First things first, fly the plane.

lized fashion while we diagnose the problem. It is only then that we can navigate a new course and communicate it to all involved.

Let's look at this theory in action with both Machine X and our weight-loss project.

We have ideated, selected, planned and communicated an innovative change in operating procedure for Machine X. With all of the requisite steps accomplished, we push the proverbial 'go' button and begin implementing the change. We have taken extraordinary care to measure the output and quality of the product exiting the machine, and before long, we notice some fluctuation and variability in the exiting product. This variability is beyond the previously determined acceptable range. What do we do now?

Our possible actions include shutting down the machine, reverting to the previous process and continuing the operation while hoping the problem resolves itself.

Shutting down the machine while we investigate causation is the most prudent, and least risky, action. It's possible that our investigation will discover extraneous influences (such as environment, faulty recording equipment, and so on) that, once remedied, will allow the innovation to be successful. It's also possible that the investigation will show that the change was too drastic and perhaps a smaller implemented change will still drive benefit, albeit on a smaller scale. It's also possible that the investigation will show that the change, despite all the planning and testing, simply will not work. Regardless, shutting down the machine will allow for the maximum flexibility pending the investigation and the least risk of an overreaction or inappropriate reaction.

We are flying the plane in a stabilized fashion while we attempt to remedy the problem. Our investigation will then provide a future direction for our innovative change, which we will then communicate out to all involved parties.

Our second option is the classic overreaction. Simply concluding that the change doesn't work without the empirical and objective data is relying on assumption in the worst possible way. Essentially, we are giving up and ceding control. Whatever happens next will probably not be in our control and an adverse consequence will be the most likely result. Even if our investigation (after previously shutting down) would have shown an unplanned fatal flaw causing a reversion to the original operating process, we have still maintained control and will probably have another opportunity to affect future changes. But when we give up, we are no longer flying the plane. And if the pilot is no longer flying the plane, who is? And who knows where it will go or in what condition it will get there?

Our third option is denial. While it is possible that the deviation is simply an anomaly not requiring any action, it is much more probable that there is something tangible causing the deviation. We need to find out what is causing the deviation so we can remedy the situation. We certainly cannot continue producing an out-of-range product in the hopes that it will fix itself. What about the cost of this unusable product? If the pilot doesn't take action to stabilize the plane, opting instead to let the plane right itself, he will probably find himself in a starring role in the next National Transportation Safety Board (NTSB) accident report.

For a more personal example, let's look at our weight-loss project.

Our erstwhile overweight person has ideated, selected, planned and communicated his idea for beginning his weight-loss journey; he has decided he will ride his bicycle to-and-from work twice a week. Four weeks later, he has lost a negligible amount of weight. This significantly deviates from his planning. What should he do now?

His possible options include stopping the cycling, continuing the cycling while he investigates why he is not losing weight, and increasing the frequency of his cycling commuting.

Stopping the cycling without any additional information is giving up. This person hasn't investigated any of the potential causes for the deviation and is ceding control of the process. He is no longer flying the plane and he has virtually no likelihood of being successful in his goal. How will he lose the necessary weight if he's no longer in control?

Continuing the cycling while investigating is the most prudent and least risky of the choices. Unlike the Machine X example, there is no harm in continuing the cycling at the planned frequency. With the investigation, he might find that he needs to alter his diet as well as continuing cycling; that he needs to increase the frequency of his cycling and/or that he needs to supplement the cycling with other exercise. He might also find that there are extraneous factors that are preventing success. These factors could include work-related or other stress, not feeling well some of the days, and so on. In other words, he is continuing to fly the plane in a stabilized fashion while he works on a remedy for the deviation. He has maintained control of the process and the change leading to a probable positive outcome in future.

Adding frequency without the requisite investigation is an overreaction. He doesn't don't know why he hasn't lost his planned weight, so how does he know that adding frequency will solve the problem? If we recall 5-Why, sometimes the issue that we think is the issue is not the issue at all. If our lack of weight loss is caused by stress, might we be adding fuel to the fire by increasing frequency? Might we be risking burnout by doing too much in uncertain conditions? While we are still in control of our plane, we are not responding to the real problem and we are very likely in danger of exasperating the issue leading to quitting and loss of control.

Key Takeaways:
1) *Changes from evaluation/assessment need to be looked at through the prism of degree.*
2) *Not all deviations will require mass changes and/or alterations.*
3) *Always be prepared to abort the mission if the conditions truly warrant it.*
4) *Ensure that the level of corrective action is appropriate to the degree and conditions of the deviation.*

✝ WRAPPING IT ALL UP ✝

We have explored our Nifty-Nine creative principles and how best to use them in our idea-generation phase. We have considered the role of bias creep and have devised strategies to eliminate or minimize its impact while selecting ideas to pursue. We have taken a closer look at change management, Changistics and the role of planning and communicating.

But it doesn't stop there. All the best planning, communicating and change strategizing are insufficient for sustainable and profitable innovation. It doesn't matter if the profitability is organizational, expressed in dollars, pounds, euros and yen or if it is personal profit earned through personal project success; the purpose of everything can be expressed in the language of profit.

Innovation and execution are all about successfully implementing the ideation and change to create these sustainable and profitable results. It is not a static phase requiring any less vigilance than the previous phases. In fact, it requires more vigilance. There is much more at stake during this phase. We need to use all of the tools we previously employed to ensure that, as we encounter the speed bumps, we can evaluate and respond accordingly. It won't be easy and will require considerable effort, but the returns will be well worth it, both personally and professionally.

And then we will truly be able to aviate, navigate and communicate... for success!

✝ADDENDUM A✝

CHANGISTICS IN ACTION – WHITE PAPER

Innovative Change Leadership Drives Company to Success
(Revised version published by Wiley Periodicals Inc., February 27, 2013)

MOE GLENNER

One organization turned around an ailing division by identifying the personal returns on investment that motivated its workforce and then crafting a strong "change chain" that linked the opening of two-way communications, a patient approach to generating sincere interest at all levels, and a recognition program to stoke enthusiasm.

When organizations are intent on changing the status quo, those who lead must be familiar with the dynamics of the change process. Not every change will lead to success; change can just as easily lead to disappointment. Ensuring that objectives are met in a change initiative requires understanding employees' needs — that is, the personal returns on investment they expect in exchange for their time, talents, and effort. With that information in hand, managers can create a chain of success composed of these essential links: Open communication, genuine interest, and widespread enthusiasm. At the transportation division of one Midwestern metals processing firm, this approach enabled the division leader to reenergize his workforce, reduce tardiness and absenteeism, and turn a money-losing enterprise into a profitable one.

Successful change initiatives do not occur in a vacuum. They are not isolated events. Any successful, enduring change initiative is the result of linked steps and events, with each link building a momentum that ultimately leads to the desired objective. Like the links in a steel chain, these links create chains — chains of change.

These chains can lead to a disappointing outcome — in which case the steps that were employed could be called part of a change-failure chain — or a beneficial result, in the case of a change success chain. In both instances, if managers were to break a link by doing something differently, they would probably affect the final outcome. Naturally, the goal for management would be to break the links in a potential change-failure chain and support the ones in a change success chain.

Identifying a Need for a Change Success Chain

The management of a large metals-processing company, headquartered in northern Indiana, US, learned the importance of taking employees' personal returns on change investments into account when they decided to improve the operations of their transportation division.

Corporate headquarters comprises three plants within five miles of one another and represents half the company's total shipping volume. While technically a separate company, the company's transportation division owes most of its business to serving the larger organization. This business handles inbound shipments of raw steel coils and outbound shipments of processed coils and steel plate product. The northern Indiana facility ships to a wide range of automotive, agricultural, and industrial customers scattered within a 400- to 600-mile radius. All the transportation functions are handled by a team of ten people: dispatchers, scale clerks, back-office clerks, and managers. As the frontline team members, the dispatchers and scale clerks are under the most pressure, because they must juggle the demands of the sales department, plant operations, and a fleet composed of independent contractor truck drivers and carriers.

The transportation division had an annual budget of $5 to $10 million, but consistently posted losses of more than $100,000, which attracted the attention of senior management. A series of poor-to-average managers had contributed to a general lack of initiative among the workforce. The team was overworked and disillusioned. Absenteeism and tardiness ran high, even among the managerial staff. Orders frequently were not shipped on time, leading to dissatisfied customers and an increasingly irate sales team. Daily production meetings of transportation, plant operations, and sales management personnel degenerated into finger-pointing blame fests, with transportation bearing the brunt of the accusations. Team-inspired initiatives to resolve the issues being faced were routinely ignored because management's attention was consumed with putting out daily "fires". The only time anyone seemed happy was at home-time.

Senior management hired a new director of transportation in the hope of turning the division around. The new director had considerable transportation and logistics experience. More important, unlike the previous directors, he was approachable, willing to listen, and ready to act on the initiatives that were brought before him. He understood the need to build a change success chain. And he also realized that to do so, he would have to make his workforce understand that they stood to gain from any improvement that the division achieved.

Focusing On Personal Returns on Investment

The success of any change initiative is predicated on the affected team members realizing their end of a grand bargain — and what they stand to gain from it. When the initiative is conceived and initially communicated, the team leader/employer is asking for the team members/employees to act on the initiative and start the change. The team members will most likely be willing to invest their time, emotion, skills, and effort to effectuate change if, as in any investment, they can expect a return. Unlike the traditional return on investment (ROI), which is strictly financial, team members' returns are more personal. Such a personal return on investment (PROI) can include not only increased financial compensation, but also recognition (either as a team and/or as a subject matter expert), opportunity (future project and/or promotion), and additional benefits (more vacation, flex-time, and so on).

In a traditional employer-employee relationship, the interpretation of this bargain has always been very different: The employer provides the job and expects the employee to do the job competently, with the return being the job itself and nothing more, except at the employer's discretion. Even in a challenging economy, however, there is considerable demand for the services of experienced and competent employees who are less willing to accept this traditional model. Understanding this, such progressive companies as Google and SAP provide a variety of previously unthinkable benefits and perks to their employees in return for their continued personal investment in organizational initiatives.

Building the Links of a Change Success Chain

Once employees are given incentives to support a change initiative, they must fully grasp all the work that will be necessary to make the change successful. Success is not an isolated event but, rather, a series of linked events and actions. Therefore, understanding the most important links in a change success chain becomes paramount. They are communication, interest, and enthusiasm.

Opening Up Avenues of Communication

Aware of the need for open communication, and drawing upon his previously successful experience, the new director of the transportation division embarked on a plan to foster two-way communication with his entire staff. He met with each employee in the transportation division, selected members of the sales team, and selected middle managers in purchasing and plant operations. His goal was to understand each person better, the role that each of them played, and their perceptions of the transportation division. With the big picture taking shape, he created a flow chart to illustrate the specific activities and responsibilities of every member of the transportation team. This exercise proved beneficial in actively engaging each member of the team and immediately opening the communications door. The flow chart also helped the new director to understand each member of his team, specifically the goals that they wanted to achieve.

All this engagement had a swift and positive effect on the morale of team members. Suddenly, someone was listening to them, and now they felt like contributors. Ideas started to be communicated and openly discussed within the division. Although the new director's authority was unquestioned, a true sense of team spirit started to evolve. The members of the transportation team were realizing an important PROI — recognition. They were being recognized as more than just employees, they felt like valued contributors to a better team.

The new director wanted to bring in a new technology platform to make the team more efficient and more responsive. This transportation management system (TMS) would pull order, lane, and rate information from the company's legacy operating system and marry it with core carriers to dispatch seamlessly all company-directed outside loads. The system also would allow for the development of customized algorithms to choose carriers according to a prioritized list of factors, including carrier lane rates, carrier safety record, past performance, and equipment availability. In addition, the system had additional modules for carrier management, rate analysis, and request for pricing (RFP) management.

Unfortunately, previous management had tried to implement a competing system and every step of that implementation was terribly botched. There was no real communication of objectives and goals, no continuous communication or active solicitation of ideas and suggestions. Ultimately, there was no success. Although the new TMS sounded good on paper, something different would be required for a successful implementation.

Understanding that this initiative would drastically change the operating procedures currently in place and increase workload until portions of it were implemented, the new director:
- Actively courted opinion on the TMS through frequent personal meetings
- Considered all ideas equally and without favoritism
- Made sure employees knew that any objections would be considered without penalty or reprisal
- Publicly recognized individual progress and contributions to both the rest of the team and to senior management
- Nominated achievers for public recognition at on-site executive meetings and in the company-wide newsletter

Through these steps, which some might consider to be 'over-communicating' to his team, he ensured that there would be no confusion regarding the initiative, its objectives, and most important, its progress. Moreover, the new director did not limit his communications to the TMS project. He also solicited employees' opinions and suggestions on other areas besides the TMS through weekly team meetings and weekly wrap-up emails to everyone on the transportation team. To further create a pleasant and energizing environment in which employees would be comfortable sharing their ideas, he encouraged the celebration of birthdays and other special occasions with fanfare.

Turning Passive Interest into Active Interest

With the transportation team members feeling like important and empowered contributors, individuals quickly communicated problems without fear of being ignored and openly exchanged ideas, not only with the new director but also with the other members of their team. Absences and tardiness dropped significantly and, in general, the team appeared happier. These developments resulted in improved relations not only among team members, but also between the transportation division and the other sectors of the organization.

The director had understood that the two primary PROIs that most employees wanted were "to be heard" and to feel like a contributor. And he delivered them. But even though most of the team members were actively interested in the initiative, there were still a few holdouts. Although these individuals were not doing anything to oppose the change, they expressed only cursory interest in it and did not do anything to support it proactively. Unlike the others, they did not ask any questions or seek to learn more about the change.

Rather than punish these holdouts for not fully supporting the TMS initiative, the new director continued to communicate with them by paying them extra attention. He realized that the holdouts' lack of active interest could have been because they did not yet fully trust him. By patiently working with these employees and spending more time with them, he helped lay the groundwork for a breakthrough. In the interim, he considered even their cursory interest as a positive.

The director reasoned that, for these members of the team, a valued PROI would be a reduced workload. As the efficiencies of the TMS kicked in, the dispatch and back-office workload started to drop. Thus, it became easier to manage the workload, and the TMS reporting functions made it easier to address anomalies in carrier rates, routing, and driver pay. Under the old system, discovering and solving such anomalies took considerable time and effort. Now team members could use many of the new reporting functions to speed through the processes. Additionally, the report data were significantly more accurate than previously. Slowly, the sceptics started to engage with the system and even began recommending adjustments to make it even more efficient. With this more active engagement, their passive interest was transformed into active interest.

Stoking Enthusiasm

The new initiative started producing immediate and tangible results. Carriers were being dealt with efficiently, bids and quotes were automated, and less time was needed to manage the transportation segment actively. Additionally, the TMS created robust competition for traffic by opening up traffic lanes to bidding from new carriers. This newly competitive environment created a downward trend for carrier-submitted lane bids. This resulted in 10% savings (versus the pre-TMS operation) on the average lane, with the more competitive lanes showing savings of 20% on their rates. Although the results were largely driven by the TMS, the changes in workflow necessary to implement new processes would not have taken hold without the director's understanding of change dynamics. Without the team feeling empowered and important to the division's success, any attempt to implement change would probably have met the fate of previous failed efforts.

The results of the completed dispatch module energized the team members and made them excited about the potential savings that could be achieved with the implementation of the remaining modules. Tracking charts were created and posted so that everyone in the division could actively monitor the progress of the changes. Continuous improvement suggestions were frequently communicated both to the director and within the team, leading to refinements that made the changes even more effective.

After an initial three months of beta testing, the division's losses were halted and it was able to post monthly profits of $10,000 to $20,000. Although these were modest gains, they represented the first time that the department had ever posted a profit. These results served to increase the overall level of enthusiasm and excitement throughout the transportation division. Much of the credit went to the director for fostering a true spirit of open communication. Consistent with his previous actions, the director passed along the credit to his team.

The CEO of the parent organization noticed these results and wanted to recognize the director publicly. Knowing that the results were obtained only through the combined efforts of the team members, the director asked that a key member of the team be recognized instead. The transportation team members selected the lead dispatcher to be recognized, personally, by the CEO and the president of the company at the following board of directors meeting.

Results Lead to Next Steps

After a full year of experience with the TMS, the transportation division posted a profit of $250,000. Absences and late arrivals had fallen significantly, without need of managerial crackdowns. The transportation team members were excited to come to work and knew that an unexcused absence or late arrival would hurt the team's overall performance. To reward the team members for their contributions, the director sought, and received permission, to give them significant year-end bonuses.

With the boost in the division's credibility, new projects, including long-overdue safety and compliance reorganizations and fleet maintenance software redesigns, were green-lighted with full budgetary and management support. Year two in the new director of transportation's tenure saw a doubling of profit from the previous year, and year three is on pace to increase threefold. The team is operating efficiently and smartly and is fully motivated to improve even further.

The success of the technology project freed up time to address several other serious issues proactively, such as improving safety records, maintenance handling, and inter-company relationships, specifically with sales and purchasing. Success breeds confidence, and confidence breeds continued improvement and better results. Although some of these additional projects are still ongoing, early results are encouraging and the team's motivation is continuing to feed off these successes.

Regardless of industry or mandate, any organization can apply the following lessons to help ensure the success of a change chain:

- *Communicate, communicate, communicate.* The enemy of confusion and fear is frequent and clear communication. Team leaders and managers must communicate the goals and objectives of any initiative effectively. They must be willing to listen carefully and openly and dispel any fears about retaliation regarding what they are told. They must encourage respectful discussion and disagreement. The results of this engagement will benefit not only the team members, but also the organization as a whole.

- *Understanding and then delivering on personal drivers is the key to buy-in.* Workers at every level want to be heard and feel they are important to the team. They all want to contribute in a meaningful way and want their efforts (their personal investment) to generate a return. When managers help ensure employees' basic PROIs, they gain the credibility to initiate and implement changes with the buy-in of the team.

- *Even passive interest is good interest.* Even employees who have only a passive interest in the change effort have a desire for a PROI — the belief that going along with the initiative, even if they do not fully buy into it, could lead to something more. Full buy-in is ideal, but it does not have to be immediate. The approach to winning over a workforce should be viewed as a marathon rather than a sprint. Passive interest also means that pushback or other barriers to the continued success of the initiative are unlikely.

- *Recognize the achievers publicly.* The most desired personal return on investment is the need for acknowledgment of a job well done. Managers can start by sincerely thanking contributors for their efforts and telling them that they did a great job. Such acknowledgement should be followed by public recognition whenever possible. This can take many forms, including recognition during team, managerial, or executive meetings and in departmental or company-wide newsletters; awards; and additional compensation in the form of salary increases and bonuses. Taking such steps to recognize those who are responsible for the day-to-day work engenders good feelings and a sense of satisfaction that deliver a PROI.

- *Encourage enthusiasm and excitement on the job.* The key to a team's enthusiasm and excitement is its manager's personal level of enthusiasm and excitement. Does this project deliver on the manager's PROI? If it does, then that manager is likely to be energized about the project. Enthusiasm and excitement is contagious. It cannot help but spread to the team, provided they are getting their PROI. The reverse is also true, however. If the project does not deliver on the manager's PROI, he or she will not be genuinely enthusiastic or excited about motivating the rest of the team. If the manager tries to keep up appearances by putting on a happy face, the team members will soon see beyond the façade. Not only will their morale plummet, but the manager's credibility will be undermined as well.

A focus on the ultimate results and not on the process used to achieve them is a mistake commonly made in many initiatives, especially technology-driven ones. But there are no shortcuts in the change success chain. Once one process is improved via a well thought-out chain of events, it will be easier to hammer out additional projects to achieve even greater successes. When employees at all levels feel they are getting a fair PROI of time and talent, they can make their organization's change chain stretch as far as their vision takes them.

ADDENDUM B

(Originally published in The Huffington Post, 11 January, 2013)

Gun Control Change We Can Believe In

As we ring in a new year, we remain shocked and saddened by the tragedy in Newtown, Connecticut. The public has responded by sounding a call to action, Vice President Biden has been tasked with finding a better way forward and, amid controversy, prominent anti-gun voices such as former congresswoman and Tucson shooting victim Gabrielle Giffords, have met with the families of the newest victims.

Every tragic incident is subsequently followed by calls for gun-control change. The politicians quickly pick up the baton and legislative bills are crafted at local and national level to address gun control. Newtown has been no different, with the Senate, vice president Biden and President Obama determined to change the laws, ostensibly to protect the public. While this is indeed a noble goal, a closer look at successful and enduring change management is necessary to predict the likelihood of its success.

Yet, state after state has passed laws allowing concealed weapons in public. All this is in the context of fewer shooting deaths overall. Are we safer now or more at risk? Do we have a gun-control issue or are they isolated incidences of "guns don't kill people, people kill people"? In the interest of full-disclosure, a disclaimer: I am not anti-gun and I believe in the sanctity of the Second Amendment with its right to bear arms, but I have always strongly questioned the inclusion of weaponry that goes beyond personal protection and/or hunting.

As a change-management consultant, I've found successful change is predicated on a three-step process: plan, communicate, execute. All three steps are critical to the probability of change success. Assuming that we want to implement a successful and enduring gun-control change law, let's apply these three critical steps.

Step 1: Plan
Any plan must include an honest assessment of the situation; the proposed scope of the change; probable and likely risks with implementing the plan or with failure of the plan; and the team charged with conceiving, implementing and executing the change. This is necessarily predicated on identification of the real issue and catalyst for the proposed change. The planning stage must also address how support will be generated, including providing personal returns for the investments of those affected.

In regards the gun issue, what is the real problem? Is it access? Is it legality of certain guns and ammunition? Is it screening for mental illness? Is it all of the above? The problem must be succinctly identified before a plan can be fashioned. For gun-control change to be effective, it must first be realistic and enforceable in scope. It must successfully be able to balance the Second Amendment right to bear arms, with restricting access to weaponry that goes well beyond. It must address the reality of special interest groups (such as the National Rifle Association (NRA)) adamantly opposing any new restrictions and the realistic threat to politicians that choose to ignore the special interest pressure. More importantly, it must find a way to gain majority support across a diverse population. While a law can be rammed through without majority support, it won't be successful in its ultimate goals without it. Finally, it must concede that it is impossible to prevent a tragedy from occurring again, but the new legislation will make its occurrence much less likely.

Sadly, current legislation being proposed is little more than a public relations stunt to make it appear that someone is doing something. If the assumption is that semi-automatic guns are the culprit for the recent tragedies, does exempting a large class of these weapons make this law practically successful? Also, does exempting current ownership of these weapons significantly alter the current situation? While the thought process is likely one of "better to get something than nothing," the argument should be, "let's get something that actually makes a significant change." More practically, this law, even if passed, won't reduce the likelihood of another Newtown. In fact, sales of semi-automatic weapons were sharply higher following the tragedy. People are anticipating a whiplash reaction and want to protect themselves from this reactive force. If anything, the sceptre of this legislation has had an opposite affect and the legislation hasn't even been debated yet, let alone passed.

The currently proposed legislation is an example of planning failure. While it is limited in scope, it is fatally limited. It also doesn't have majority support nor does it address how its supporters will respond to both special-interest challenges and to the current situation. In this case, it is better to have no legislative response than a poor, ineffective legislative response. A better solution might be to engage the special interest groups which also want to avoid repeats of Newtown. While there has been historic opposition to restrictions on semi-automatic weaponry, perhaps there can be movement in this direction with guarantees towards protection of overall Second Amendment rights. After all, hunting or personal protection doesn't really require the ability to shoot multiple rounds in seconds.

Step 2: Communicate
Any change initiative requires honest, relevant and timely communication between the sponsor, team leaders, team members and those affected. The key is honest communication. Communications that herald bad news, setbacks or failures cannot lead to a 'punish the messenger' response. Effective gun-change legislation requires clear and honest communication as to intent, scope and reach. If the legislation is intended to reduce drastically the public's access to semi-automatic weapons and nothing more, then this must be communicated. If the legislation is also intended to guarantee Second Amendment rights as far as handguns and concealed weapons, this too must be clearly communicated.

Unfortunately, the term "honest politician" is now considered an oxymoron. There is a distinct shortage of politician credibility. We have been trained by past communications and actions not to believe anything that a politician says. Furthermore, most of us tend to believe that the politician probably has ulterior motives behind the legislation. In other words, even if the politicians were to really, truly communicate on this issue, we might not believe them. Is there hope, then, of passing effective gun-control change? Yes, but it will take a real and sizeable majority across party, geographical and demographical lines for us to consider believing the communication. Without this, it all might sound good, but we won't be buying whatever they are selling.

Step 3: Execute
Finally, the change initiative must be executed according to plan. While no initiative ever proceeds exactly as planned, the ability to 'roll with the changes' and respond to changing landscapes is key to seeing the change initiative through. Probable and potential changes should be addressed at the planning stage, communicated throughout the initiative, and then executed appropriately.

If the gun-control plan (legislation) is intended to reduce drastically the public availability and access to semi-automatic weaponry, then the scope and reach must reflect this in the planning stage; must be communicated to the public prior to, and throughout, the legislative process; and then must be acted upon by the legislators with their affirmative voting. Finally, it must be signed into law and then enforced with the full resources provided and available to it. Anything less will be an execution failure that directly results in a change failure.

We can only hope that the current attention being given to this issue is not just 'yesterday's news' and/or an attempt to mollify the public. If successful and enduring change is to take hold, Gabrielle Giffords' struggles and voice must be heard in the effort to push for the solution. We should also be encouraged by the efforts of the vice president to solicit as many disparate and diverse voices on this issue, provided the opinions are seriously considered. The real solution must be inclusive and not exclusive of any of the affected constituencies (in other words, all of us).

While meaningful gun-control legislation might not prevent another Newtown, it will dramatically decrease the likelihood of it happening again. And that's a change we can, and should, all believe in, regardless of political, geographic or demographic affiliation.

(Second article, originally published in The Huffington Post, January 17, 2013)

Where Is 'Change We Can Believe In'?

With President Obama's re-inauguration around the corner, Americans should be looking forward to more of the meaningful change he promised in his first election. Unfortunately, the changes we received included an even more intense partisan environment, quick fix 'bandages' and real changes endlessly deferred. Surveys continuously and overwhelmingly show Americans supported compromise when it came to the recent fiscal cliff crisis. Perhaps what we were really saying is that we didn't want a real solution, but rather for the immediate problem to go away. How many of us are living in the United States of Denial?

The problem is, many of us don't want change if it's accompanied by any degree of pain. I believe many of us look at the each political crisis as an artificially placed fear to spur political concessions. We don't really think any repercussions could actually take place. We know that something will be worked out. We believe we will resume our scheduled life once the scandal of the day blows over.

Our fiscal arm is hanging by a thread and we accept the equivalent of slapping a bandage on as a viable solution. Sure, the fiscal cliff has been diverted, but we still have the national debt ceiling and looming insolvencies of Medicare and Social Security. Denying these problems, and refusing to make sincere efforts to remedy them, isn't going to make them disappear.

When we were children, we played kick-the-can and the can would be kicked further down the street until it was lost or we got bored. As adults, we're still playing that game – but with much higher stakes. We don't want to pick up the can and end the game; instead, we prefer to kick it away and deal with it later. We attempt to avoid confrontation, and we suggest compromise is the answer to our problems.

Compromise can indeed be a useful tool, even in politics. However, recent political compromises have failed to introduce lasting change. We say we want changes to our flawed political arena, but in today's hyper-partisan world, we (and, by extension, our elected officials) aren't willing to concede anything, making real change unlikely to occur. Yet, we keep electing them and then blame them when nothing gets done. It's a never-ending game of dodge ball, Washington style.

Effective change relies on honest, relevant and constant communication between the change team (in this case, our elected officials) and those affected by the change (the rest of us). Tragically, many consider the phrase "honest politician" an oxymoron. We tend to punish honest communication because it's not what we want to hear. Thus, we actively encourage dishonest political communication, as long as the message meets our approval. In fact, the continuous election cycle guarantees dishonest political communication, since the politicians are always running for re-election. The politicians may indeed be upstanding citizens and otherwise honest people, but their communication is anything but. The simple truth is this: we American citizens have created and propagate the career politician.

If we truly want meaningful and enduring change, we must start by being honest with ourselves. We must be more informed. We must demand honest political communication without finger pointing. We must stop punishing honest communication. But most of all, we must demand and enforce accountability.

In most business organizations, if 'Nero were fiddling while Rome was burning', Nero would be terminated by the board of directors. If government were a business, we would adamantly insist on accountability. We wouldn't stand for the continued spending of money we don't actually have, so why do we tolerate, and even encourage, it with our government? As stockholders, we demand accountability. As customers, we demand accountability. Excepting major scandals, as voters, we don't really demand accountability. With relatively few exceptions, we keep voting the same people back in. Effective change relies on accountability, where each member of the team is accountable to every other member, but more importantly to those affected by the end result. If the incumbents can't, or won't, get it done, we must relieve them of their positions.

Of course, these changes wouldn't be easy or immediate, but the return on the investment would be great; namely an end to Washington's games of dodge ball and kick-the-can and real movement towards a better tomorrow.

REFERENCES

I have taken considerable care and effort to credit any direct quotes used in this work. However, much of my knowledge and background has been influenced, directly and indirectly, by the works of many before me. As such, I wanted to credit those authors/works in appreciation for their influence and spurring of new ideas and directions.

Collins J, Hansen M , *Great by Choice*, Harper-Collins, New York, NY, 2011

Berkun, S, *The Myths of Innovation*, O'Reilly Media, Sebastopol, CA, 2007

Matson M, *Innovate or Die*, Paradigm Press, Royal Oak, MI, 1996

Burkus D, *The Myths of Creativity*, Jossey-Bass, San Francisco, CA, 2014

Richard C, *Certain to Win*, Xlibris Corporation, 2004

de Bono, E, *Creativity Workout*, Ulysses Press, Berkeley, CA, 2008

Adair J, *The Art of Creative Thinking*, Kogan Page US, Philadelphia, PA, 2009

Govindarajan V, Trimble C, *Reverse Innovation*, Harvard Business School Publishing, Boston, MA 2012

Babineaux R, Krumboltz J, *Fail Fast, Fail Often*, Penguin Group USA, New York, NY, 2013

Burkus J, *Inside Adobe's Innovation Kit*, Harvard Business Review, February 23, 2015

Raymundo O, *How to Build a Secret Army of Innovators*, Inc.com, December 12, 2014

Innovation Revolution, Adobe Life Magazine, 2015

Schoenberger C, *Trying to understand the science behind strategy*, Capital Ideas, Chicago Booth School of Business, Spring 2014

Schrager J, Madansky A, B*ehavioral strategy: a foundational view*, Journal of Strategy and Management, 6:1, 2013

Smith D, *Twitter's CEO used to be a professional comedian – here's how improv comedy helped him be a better leader*, BusinessInsider.com, February 25, 2015

Stone B, *How to Run Your Company Like an Improv Group, by Twitter CEO Disk Costolo*, BloombergBusiness, April 11, 2013

Schurenberg E, *Twitter CEO Disk Costolo: What I've Learned*, Inc.com, 17 May 2013

Inam A, MIT, *Navigating Ambiguity: Comedy Improvisation as a Tool for Urban Design Pedagogy and Practice*, Journal for Education in the Built Environment, 5:1, July, 2010

Chamorro-Premuzic T, *Why Brainstorming Works Better Online*, Harvard Business Review, April 2, 2015

AN INTRODUCTION TO MOE GLENNER

Moe Glenner is a highly acclaimed thought leader on personal and professional leadership, change management and innovation. He is the author of *Selfish Altruism: Managing & Executing Successful Change Initiatives* and has been seen on ABC, NBC, CBS & Fox and has had many articles on creativity, leadership and change management published in magazines such as Inc., *Bloomberg Businessweek*, *The Huffington Post*, *Internet Truckstop* and *inBusiness*. Moe is also a frequent contributor on LinkedIn Pulse.

Moe is an in-demand corporate creativity consultant and frequent keynote, breakout and workshop speaker. His work is always informative, interesting and communicated in an entertaining and memorable style.

Moe holds a Bachelor of Arts (BA) in History from Northeastern Illinois University, a Masters of Business Administration (MBA) from Lake Forest Graduate School of Management (Lake Forest, IL), Lean Six Sigma Black Belt Certification from Villanova University (Philadelphia, PA) and is a professional general aviation pilot.

Moe has served in a number of senior management and consulting roles for multi-national, multi-billion dollar enterprises as well as mid-range and entrepreneurial ventures. Moe continues to lead and transform management and corporate cultural functions through his innovation initiatives. These initiatives have resulted in multi-million dollar cost reductions, creating and building of profit centers and the start of corporate creativity workshops.

CONCISE ADVICE LAB